HEALED NOT BROKEN

Based on a True Story

KYNA BRYN

ISBN 979-8-88751-876-3 (paperback)
ISBN 979-8-88751-878-7 (digital)

Copyright © 2023 by Kyna Bryn

All rights reserved. No part of this publication may be reproduced, distributed, or transmitted in any form or by any means, including photocopying, recording, or other electronic or mechanical methods without the prior written permission of the publisher. For permission requests, solicit the publisher via the address below.

Christian Faith Publishing
832 Park Avenue
Meadville, PA 16335
www.christianfaithpublishing.com

Printed in the United States of America

To my beautiful sister in Christ, Carole A. Hiatt. I thank the Lord for placing her in my life. Carole was the perfect example of what a woman of faith truly looks like. She was caring and shined the light of Jesus everywhere she went.

To my beautiful daughter. I pray that you continue to pursue your relationship with the Lord. Every day is an opportunity to draw near Him. I am so blessed to be your mom. Know that you are loved beyond measure. Today, always, and forever.

CONTENTS

Chapter 1: My Name Is Zara 1
Chapter 2: The Search 13
Chapter 3: The Encounter 21
Chapter 4: The Adventure 29
Chapter 5: The Signs and Wonders 44
Chapter 6: The Freedom 59
Chapter 7: The Miracle 77
Chapter 8: The Challenge 95
Chapter 9: The Blessings 113
Chapter 10: The Work 128
Chapter 11: The Start 134
Chapter 12: The Demonic 153
Chapter 13: The Faith 174
Chapter 14: The Heart 191
Chapter 15: The Now 200

CHAPTER 1

MY NAME IS ZARA

There is just no way to describe the events that have happened in my life these past five years without using the words, "ONLY HAPPENS IN THE MOVIES," "IMPOSSIBLE MADE POSSIBLE," and "MIRACLES." Even the word, "BLESSED," or perhaps the words, "DREAMS COME TRUE"—all of which I never thought I, myself, Zara Banks, would ever be saying. The question is, How much are you willing to believe? The things I have witnessed and that have happened range from a supernatural overabundance of blessings financially and even real physical healings only God could do to actually seeing demons manifest and people set free of torment.

I have witnessed light come and darkness leave in deliverances as if I was literally standing on a movie set. I am honestly not sure if anyone will ever believe me. However, my reply is simple! I am saying that I don't have to or want to make you believe anything. I really have no interest in trying to strong-arm anyone to believe that Jesus is the way and that God is not dead. I am simply sharing what happened to me and where I am now because I believe both of those statements.

The year 2018 is going to be hard to put into words, but I am going to try my best. I will be honest and share all of it. I do not want to spend time rehashing too much of the past or explaining what and where I have come from. Not because I don't believe it's relevant to this story but because I have already shared my story in a book that goes into great detail about my past. The truth is that if you knew me yesterday, you should spend some time with me today because I am growing every moment of my life. The book I shared my story in is called *Broken Not Shattered* by the author Kyna Bryn. The woman in that story seriously is not the same woman before you today. My name is still Zara, but my heart, thoughts, and life will never be the same.

This story actually begins where *Broken Not Shattered* left off. So I suppose we will just call it book two, but if you didn't read book one, no worries. This book is loaded! The first book was just me exposing every dirty little secret I had, exposing all of my mistakes, things that happened to me, and lessons learned throughout my life. Now with all of that behind me, I am excited to share with you what God did to a life that became truly surrendered to Him. I've learned and continue to learn what denying myself truly means every single day.

For many years, I didn't sleep well, and so I entertained this specific dream. You could even call it a fantasy because I would think about it often. I would imagine that I had three wishes, and I could ask for anything, and it would come true. For the longest time, my first wish was to have ten duffel bags each filled with $1 million cash. I'm not sure why I wanted the money in duffel bags. I suppose my thought was that it would be easier to transport and hide the money in them.

My second wish was that my body would be in the best shape. My idea of best shape was having no stretch marks, teeth straight, and six-pack killer abs. I admit I would stipulate that wish with still being able to eat anything I wanted without gaining weight back. It was my fantasy, and I like good food. What can I say?

My third wish was the only wish that would change throughout the years. I would go from having my criminal record, the mistakes of my past, wiped out; and then as years past, my wish became to know and understand God more. The third wish would bounce between the two, and I would consider the fact that with the money, I could clear up my record because I could hire an attorney and that person could help me. So knowing and understanding God became a more frequent desire.

Since I was young, I believed in Jesus Christ and was convinced beyond a reasonable doubt that He was my Lord and Savior, but I only knew one side of the relationship. I only knew me turning to Him in times of need, saying prayers every night with my daughter, and just believing that He loved me and would embrace me when I died. Even when I was an alcoholic, I believed that Jesus loved and accepted me just as I was. I occasionally did drugs, I had sex outside of marriage, and I made a lot of mistakes. I walked in sin believing that my decisions were just part of who I was, my identity. I still believe that Jesus loved me even in my mess even with my ignorance and unawareness of who I was truly created to be.

> **My dear children, I write this to you so that you will not sin. But if anybody does sin, we have an advocate with the Father-Jesus Christ, the Righteous One. He is the atoning sacrifice for our sins, and not only for ours but also for the sins of the whole world. (1 John 2:1–2 NIV)**

You can't convince me of any different. What I have come to discover and believe is the difference is that the Lord does love me as I am, but He loves me too much to leave me this way. Every day, we grow more when we surrender and pursue knowing Him. He prunes, plucks, molds, sets us on fire, and stretches us; and these are only a few of what I have experienced. God does not fit in anyone's box, and no theology is 100 percent accurate.

For me, it is crazy that we will actually argue so deeply about our beliefs that what we claim to believe doesn't even show through our words or actions. Maybe it is just me, but it seems like many of us would rather "be right" than be humble. You can be right and still be wrong with the way you say or do something. It truly boils down to the motive of your heart, which is between you and Father. Didn't Jesus pay a high price for all of us?

My only child, Bree, graduated from high school in 2017. She was getting ready to go off to college in the fall. I was single and had sold everything to pursue my dream. My heart's desire was to help others to understand they could overcome whatever life throws at them. I wanted to make my mark in this world as someone who could encourage others. It was in my heart to show that no matter what happens in your life, you just have to keep going. Get back up after being knocked down and know that with assurance, you are worth the fight. I thought that I had overcome addiction; being raped, molested, and abused; and being used most of my life. Not to mention the stupid dangerous situations I would put myself in.

I did know that, without the Lord, I could have never gotten where I was. I still believe that to this day. It was my dream to help others, but inside, there was still this place in me that wanted to be successful. I didn't want to have to fight, strive, or depend on anyone to help me make ends meet again. I just wanted to be financially stable and never have to go to another food bank or be on state assistance. It isn't wrong to want to be financially stable, but I lived believing that I would be undoubtedly happy when everything came together financially. The mindset I had was that I will find true happiness when I have money. I was choosing to live in the "when" motives rather than being thankful in the now moments. I didn't truly understand that it is in the journey, not the destination, that we can walk in peace and joy. It is in today!

I was promoting that I had finally broken the chains of addiction to alcohol and was walking in freedom. At the time, I was convinced that I had, yet I still drank and would sometimes get drunk. I thought that because I didn't do it every day, I was in control. I convinced myself of that because it helped me sleep or that I wouldn't get drunk every time; I used whatever excuse because it was just an excuse, to excuse my decisions. So, what if once in a while I went a little overboard. I mean, most of us do, right?

My ex-husband used to say that I found a reason to drink all the time. Saint Patrick's Day, drink; Fourth of July, drink; Memorial Day, drink; Labor Day, drink; Thanksgiving, drink;

Christmas, well, I think you get the point. He was right. I always drank on those holidays and more because I always had. I didn't realize I was captured by a false identity that drinking was who I was. I was wrong to think that drinking was the *normal* thing to do. I had no idea I was still a prisoner while I claimed to be free.

There were moments when I would drink too much, and I wouldn't remember things. I began to feel lost in what my purpose even was. I felt ashamed and a lot of condemnation for my actions and would feel like I wasn't enough. I would convince myself when I would drink too much that I would never do it again. I would think to myself, *I was just learning my limit* and *That was too much*. Truth be told, I had no control. I was alone, and no one saw me, yet it felt like the eyes of the world were looking directly at me and judging me.

Reflecting on it now, I know how lost I truly was. Whether I was drunk or not, smoking weed was always something I did as well. I was what most would call a "pothead," and I never saw anything wrong with that either. To be clear, I'm not dismissing the medical benefits of marijuana, but I was smoking for the high. I was only seeing it my way and not truly surrendering my life to the one who gave me life. It was like I wanted to know God and understand my purpose without realizing I was clinging to an identity and habits He never created me for. I didn't realize that even though I was pursuing Him in the only way I knew; He was actually pursuing me even more.

I have read a lot of books on how to live better or how to have more faith. "How-to" books were something I was often drawn to. I also read my Bible a lot but more when I was feeling lost because something inside me felt the answers were always there. I knew my life was about to change drastically because my daughter was leaving for college, and I was risking it all. My plan was simple, traveling all over in my travel trailer and truck doing motivational speeches and book signings. I was right: Everything in my life changed, and nothing would ever be the same, but it didn't happen the way I imagined it would.

There are things that happened to me throughout these years that have stretched me in ways I would have never even dreamed. There will be things that may sound unbelievable to you. Even though they happened to me, I admit, I still have a hard time believing them myself. I have always had this desire inside of me, almost like this knowing, because I somehow knew there was more to life than just my circumstances. I didn't understand why I couldn't seem to find a place I could call home, just somewhere I could belong and feel right or even true peace. I suppose that is why scripture tells us:

> **If the world hates you, keep in mind that it hated me first. If you belonged to the world, it would love you as its own. As it is, you do not belong to the world, but I have chosen you out of the world. That is why the world hates you. (John 15:18–19 NIV)**

We are in the world, but we are not of the world. I believe that as followers and disciples of Christ, we are challenged by not feeling as if we belong. Once we truly surrender and renew our minds in His Word, we grow to understand that we actually belong to Him. There is no better place than to finally come to the understanding that our Father truly loves us. He is for us and not against us.

I was challenged for a long time on asking why I was molested, or why both of my uncles abused me. Even though I felt as though I truly forgave them, I still didn't understand. I couldn't grasp why would God allow them to do that to me. Yet at the same time, I realized that I didn't want to drink, and I was still drinking. I had no doubt that God had not forsaken me. I believed He was with me even through the worst, but a small part of me still wondered, *Why?* As I continue to share in the next chapters, you will see how the Lord has truly revealed to me the peace, joy, and understanding He wants for all of us.

For a long time, I didn't have any answers as to why God allows tragedy, hurts, pain, and attacks. One day, as I was praying and listening to a sermon by Pastor Dan Mohler on YouTube, I had the revelation that God loved my uncles as much as He loved me. If either of them had known who they were as His sons, they would have never touched me. See, I realized that the enemy is who comes to kill, steal, and destroy, not God.

> **The thief comes only to steal and kill and destroy; I have come that they may have life, and have it to the full. (John 10:10 NIV)**

So in seeking the answer to why God would allow my uncle to molest me or my other uncle to rape and beat me, He answered me. God doesn't take away our free will. Can God stop something tragic from happening absolutely? God can do anything and everything. He is the God of the impossible. Yet He also doesn't take away our free will, which means that He loves my uncles, and although, He loves me, He wouldn't force me to stop doing something I wanted to do, such as drinking myself stupid. So then, why would He force Himself on my uncles? If they knew who they were, adopted and inheritances of the kingdom of God, sons of the King, and knew their identity, neither of them would have done anything to dishonor or hurt me. They had no idea as to who they were created to be, and neither did I. If we believe that God is real, how can we not believe that Satan is as well? My uncles had the same problem I did; their identity had been stolen, clouded, lost.

God is the only one who knows the true posture of our hearts. He desires a relationship with each and every one of us. As we seek to know Him, we discover who we are. It is not about religion. Personally, I don't like religion. It says that you must earn, be, or do things to be accepted and loved. Yet King David said it best in psalms.

> **For you created my inmost being; you knit me together in my mother's womb. (Psalm 139:13 NIV)**

How amazing is it that the God of the universe, the one who creates all things, actually took the time, love, and devotion to knit you together in your mother's womb? He planned for you. He has a purpose for you. He has set you apart as His. It wasn't just because your mom and dad came together and had sex, nope. God Himself created and designed you to be His, and His love for you is far beyond what you can grasp.

Once you just get a taste of understanding how much He desires a relationship with you, you'll never be the same. If you can focus on understanding how much He truly loves you and believe what He says, He can transform your entire life. I am not speaking from a lack of walking things out. I have a testimony to share that will rock your world and has completely transformed the way I see, the way I speak, and the way I feel about everything. I am living proof that God can do the impossible, and I am convinced He can do it for you as well.

In His Word, the Lord tells us that He has great plans for us. He wants us prosperous. He wants us to know how much He desires to be in a relationship with us. In any relationship, it takes effort and stewarding our time with each other. A husband and wife set aside time for "date nights," and in our friendships, we set time aside for coffee or meals and the like. We make calls and texts and communicate in order to "do life" together, to show love, to care for each other, and to be a part of what is happening as each day passes. Truth is God desires the same. He wants us to spend time with Him. He wants us to talk to Him, have coffee and dinner dates, and care about what His will is for our lives. In all things we do, He is with us. The question is, Are we acknowledging His presence in all we do? Are we asking Him what He wants us to do when we have big decisions or even little decisions to make? Are we asking Him for the things we need and even the things we want? Do you wonder what it looks like to truly hear from Him? One of the many huge lessons I have learned is that His plan is far better than my own.

I thought it was difficult to know if I was doing His will or my own until I realized it wasn't. It is actually crazy how easy it is when we truly desire to know Him more and we are willing to listen. When you have peace about a decision, could it be God is giving you the answer you are seeking? Could it truly be that simple? What about the times you feel like it may not be right, but it's what you want and you do it anyway? For me, that is when what I thought was going to be awesome becomes a complete disaster. I believe that we are the ones who make things way more complicated than they are by not listening to Holy Spirit and just living for what we want rather than what He wants.

> **For I know the plans I have for you, declares the Lord, plans to prosper you and not to harm you, plans to give you hope and a future. (Jeremiah 29:11 NIV)**

We also need to recognize that we are in a war. The Lord gives us full armor for a reason (see Ephesians 6:10–18). We are His soldiers, not just His children. When the Lord says come as a child, He doesn't mean come immature and ignorant. When the Lord speaks about coming to Him as a child, He means that we need to come with our faith as a child, not consumed with having to know every answer. Just simply believe. We tend to overanalyze and only believe what we see, yet Jesus tells us the following:

> **Because you have seen me, you have believed; blessed are those who have not seen and yet have believed. (John 20:29 NIV)**

> **For the wisdom of this world is foolishness in God's sight. (1 Corinthians 3:19 NIV)**

It is the good fight of faith and believing you are who God says you are, not what the world says. Above all else, we must believe Him. The true battle comes when you begin to take ahold of your true identity and not allow anything to shake you. You read that right. Life doesn't just get easier when you accept Jesus Christ as your Lord and Savior. Growing with Jesus Christ as your true foundation doesn't mean everything is going to be perfect, and you will never have another problem again. It means that you are not in this battle by yourself. You are not fighting or facing anything alone anymore. Actually, He assures us we will face hard times, but He also assures us He will never leave or forsake us. He assures us that He is our defender and has our backs. Many of us are facing the same war, but He gives us weapons. Truth is, once you realize the war you've been fighting is the darkness trying to dim your light, you see that it isn't with flesh and blood. Your eyes will be opened when you truly seek, ask, and knock.

> **Keep on asking, and you will receive what you ask for. Keep on seeking, and you will find. Keep on knocking, and the door will be opened to you. (Matthew 7:7 NLT)**

Okay, okay. How about I just share exactly what happened to me in 2018 so that you have a better understanding of where and why I am saying what I am saying. Let me start by introducing myself. My name is Zara Banks, and I am a citizen of heaven, a disciple of Jesus Christ, a mother, writer, warrior, daughter, speaker, redeemed, made new, and am finally truly free from the bondage that once had its grip on me. I have been delivered since January 20, 2018. I have been set free because of the blood of Jesus Christ. I am writing this book in order to share the events that I have witnessed and experienced with the hope that it encourages others to know there is hope, peace, freedom, and joy available right now.

My prayer is that you will be encouraged by my testimony to pursue your own intimate relationship with the creator of the universe—Our God, who longs for a relationship with you. We don't have to "clean ourselves" up before coming to Him. If we could clean ourselves up, we wouldn't even need Him. God desires and longs for you to walk in the truth of who He created you to be—to fulfill the destiny He has set out for you to fulfill. You are loved. You are worthy. You are a child of the Most High. Whether you believe it or not doesn't change these truths. I bless you and pray that the abundant mercy and grace that the Lord has shown me will become the reality in your life as well. I pray that you experience His love and grace and His peace and joy in your life "on earth as it is in heaven."

> **For God so loved the world that He gave His one and only Son, that *whoever believes in Him* shall not perish, but have eternal life. (John 3:16 New International Version)**

> **For this is how much God loved the world-he gave his one and only, unique Son as a gift. So now *everyone who believes in him* will never perish but experience ever-lasting life. (John 3:16 The Passion Translation)**

> **For God so loved the world, that he gave his only begotten Son, that *whosoever believeth in him* should not perish, but have everlasting life. (John 3:16 King James Version)**

> **For God so loved the world, that he gave his only Son, that *whoever believes in him* should not perish but have eternal life. (John 3:16 English Standard Version)**

> **For this is how God loved the world; He gave his one and only Son, so that *everyone who believes in him* will not perish but have eternal life. (John 3:16 New Living Translation)**

> **God loved the people of this world so much that he gave his only Son, so that *everyone who has faith in him* will have eternal life and never really die. (John 3:16 Contemporary English Version)**

For this is how God loved the world: He gave his unique Son so that *everyone who believes in him* might not be lost but have eternal life. (John 3:16 International Standard Version)

This is how much God loved the world: He gave his Son, his one and only Son. And this is why; so that *no one need be destroyed; by believing in him*, anyone can have a whole and lasting life. (John 3:16 The Message Bible)

CHAPTER 2

THE SEARCH

July 2017

In order to understand the year 2018, I have to take you back a little bit. I had just moved back to Indiana after spending two years in Michigan. I was starting to drink a little more often and heavier than I had been in a long time. One night, I got so intoxicated that I decided I needed to have sex. Now the crazy thing is that when I was sober, I had no interest in sex, a relationship, or even dating. Yet I found myself so drunk that I allowed something to take full authority over my mind and body.

I called someone over who I knew had a heart for me, and I just took total advantage of the man. The next morning when I woke up, I physically felt shame as if an open invitation had been sent, and shame came to just hang out and torment me. I can't explain how embarrassed and condemned I felt. Something happened to me that morning that changed my life and started me down a journey I never expected. It was as if something inside of me had broken. I could see I was not living right, and something other than me had control because I was definitely not in control.

I literally apologized to my friend, who had no regrets, but I knew this was not my story. I knew there had to be more to life. I actually locked myself down for months and just pursued getting to know God. I would say things like, "I don't understand, but I want to"; "I don't know how to know you, but I want to"; and "I can't keep doing this. Please help me." I was lost, and all I knew was that Jesus had answers, and I wasn't going anywhere until He talked to me. It was in late August when I found myself driving Bree to her first apartment near her college. I couldn't help but be excited for her. However, a part of me knew how very much I was going to miss her.

On the first night she was gone, she did end up calling me crying. She said she wasn't sure if she was ready to be on her own and that she missed me. I honestly felt like racing over to get her. I was only a forty-five-minute drive from her, but I knew she had to overcome her emotions and push through. This was her time, and all she needed to do was adjust. I was convinced she would be happy once school started and she got to know some people. Although there wasn't a dormitory on campus, her apartment was in a complex literally in the backyard of the college, and she had two roommates in the process of moving in as well. After we talked for a while and once Bree felt calmed down, she said she was going to try to get some sleep, and we said goodnight.

At first, my heart was overwhelmed to know that she was feeling the same way I was. Deep within, I wasn't sure if I was ready for her to be gone either, but this is what normal people do, right? Their kids go to college, and life just moves in this direction of school, work, and the like. Being alone gave me a lot of time to think about life and wonder what direction I should be going. All I had was an older, leaky travel trailer and an older rusted truck. I had sold what I did have, and I didn't have money in the bank or some savings to fall back on. I was blessed with a dear friend's uncle who was willing to allow me to park my trailer on his property for the time being. My thoughts were to get Bree settled in her apartment, and by late October, I would head to Florida or somewhere south to pursue my career as an author and motivational speaker.

Bree decided to go to college near the town we had lived in for eleven years back in Indiana. Once she was settled in, I touched base with my church and some of the beautiful ladies I had attended Bible studies with a few years prior. It was amazing how much support and love I received. It was such a blessing to be near my little brother, Dakota, again, as well. By this time, he had a baby and was doing good. My niece is so beautiful, and I loved being able to babysit and just get time with her. I also received an offer to speak at a couple of ladies' church events. I started to feel like things in life were really beginning to come together. I was still drinking, but I limited myself to a pint here and there at night to help me sleep. I had also started taking pain pills my mother gave me to help me sleep, as well. Honestly, I was seeking the Lord at every turn and just desperately wanted to understand my purpose.

Although money was extremely tight, I kept faith that the Lord would provide and that everything was going to be okay. As the end of September came, I truly believed I would load up everything and start heading south with my truck and travel trailer. I kept praying about what God wanted me to do, and I felt like I was supposed to stay where I was even though I didn't understand it or really want to. I really didn't have the money to travel, but I was used to taking huge leaps of faith and had no problem loading up and seeing where the Lord would lead me. However, He had other plans that I had no idea about. So I made the decision to stay put a little longer and see what happened.

October 2017

I had my first speaking event with another speaker who was also in attendance. Her name was Gem. There was something inside of me that drew me to Gem. I couldn't explain why, but I felt like I was supposed to get together with her for coffee or something, some time outside of the event. So when the opportunity was available, I invited her to get together, and she agreed to meet with me. We ended up making a date to meet at the Starbucks in Muncie, Indiana. I was excited to speak with Gem but strangely couldn't explain the excitement. Our date was set for a time in November.

I had recently gotten with a couple of ladies from the church, and they really didn't mind all of my questions about scripture. I was very focused on wanting to know and understand Jesus and who He is. One of the ladies was a leader of the women's Bible studies on Sundays, and I felt really blessed to have her in my life. Sally knew a lot about scripture and was open with me when I asked questions. I felt like we had grown a bond and formed a friendship. Plus I trusted her because she had a position in the church. She had women coming to her for mentoring and advice, so I believed most of what she said.

There were moments I would have to remind myself that Sally was just a woman and doesn't have all the answers. I couldn't help myself though. I asked a lot of questions and was hungry for truth. I was slowly being introduced to sides of the Christian world that I didn't know anything about or perhaps didn't want to know existed.

I also began meeting with Dorothy. She was an older woman from my church who was so sweet and really knew the scripture inside and out. Dorothy was a powerful example of a woman dedicated to the Lord. Plus she had never been married, had no children (she was a virgin), and was an only child. Dorothy was the last left in her family, and she was at the young age of seventy-six years old. She was also an assistant to Sally for the Bible study groups at church and had been a teacher in the area for about thirty-five years before retiring.

I really listened when Dorothy would speak because she had a peacefulness and truth in her. What she said could be backed up with scripture, and she didn't hesitate to pull out her phone Bible app and show you. I became curious about the gift of tongues and began asking questions about it. Dorothy ended up pointing me to a preacher named Andrew Wommack. She encouraged me to check out the videos on the teaching Andrew does called "Spirit, Soul, and Body."

November 2017

The day had finally come for my meeting with Gem, and I was anxious to see why I was feeling the way I was. I have met many people in my life, but this was different. It was as if I almost felt like God was placing me there to talk to this woman. As we sat down at the Starbucks and began talking, out of the blue, Gem began staring out the window. All of a sudden, she said, "Yes, Lord, yes." I was not sure what to think. I looked around, a bit confused, because I had never had anyone do anything like that before. She started saying she saw me on a pillar and that God was going to use me as a stepping stone to bring many people to Him. She said that God was going to take cuss words off my lips and that I would speak in tongues. She also added that I needed to get healthy because I would be in and out of airplanes and that I needed to get rooted like a tree. She said that God needed to be my foundation. Needless to say, my jaw about dropped to the floor, and I had no idea what to say.

My first thought was, *What the hell is happening here?* After I got home, Sally ended up calling me and asking how my meeting went. I explained that it was like a tarot card reading, and it was super strange. Sally began giggling at me and said, "Zara, Gem is a prophetess." I had no idea what she was talking about or what a prophetess even was. The whole experience blew me away. I continued to spend every second in scripture and began watching the videos from Andrew Wommack "Spirit, Soul, and Body."

I can't even begin to explain how my Bible became alive. I started understanding what I was reading as I actually began just trying to know God. Rather than just get Him to answer my cries, questions, or my wants, I really just wanted to know Him and understand what I am doing here on this earth. As I continued to study, I realized that a lot of what I had been taught was in pieces. There were little things, like, "Wives, submit to your husbands," Yes, the Bible says that. Yet the rest of that scripture is about how the husband is to love the wife as Christ loves the church. WAIT A MINUTE. HOLD THE PHONE.

I saw that I was created with value, and intentionally as were you. It was mind-blowing how the Words came alive, and I couldn't get enough. At this time, I talked to my mother often, and when I explained to her what was happening, she started calling me with scripture to go against anything I said. At one point, I felt like the Lord told me not to work, which I thought was crazy. However, I knew what I knew, and I wanted to be obedient even when it didn't make sense. My mother just ended up calling me with scripture about not being lazy. It was insane how much she wanted to prove that everything I said was wrong.

Then one day, with only $50 to my name and $500 in bills due the next day, I was on my treadmill. All of a sudden, I felt like the Lord said that my $50 belonged to Jill, a friend of mine. I literally began arguing out loud about how I couldn't be hearing right. That was the last of my money. How was I going to make any bills work out? Blah, blah. For forty-five minutes, I fought what I knew I heard in my heart. Finally, not in some joyous loving heart way either but in an upset, disobedient, angry, child-like way, I jumped off the treadmill and said, "Fine!" I didn't even change my sweaty clothes. I just got in my truck and headed to Jill's house.

When I knocked on the door, Jill was surprised to see me. I explained that I didn't understand why, but I felt like the Lord told me to give her this $50 and that I pray it blessed her. She literally started crying and explained that the amount was exactly what she needed for her bill, and she was just praying about how to pay it. I left there in awe and apologized to Father for being stubborn. I wanted and still want to be quick to listen and slow to speak when it comes to what or where I feel like the Lord wants me.

That night, I went to sleep not knowing exactly how I was going to cover my bills as if the $50 could have covered the $500 anyway, but I had peace about the whole thing. The next morning, I woke up to a random message from someone from the church who said, "Zara, while in prayer last night, the Lord told me to give you $500. I was wondering if that would be okay, and if you could come to pick up a check?"

I fell to my knees and started crying. What do you do with that? I was blown away. Things like this don't really happen, or do they?

December 2017

I spent the month digging and diving deeper into my Bible. I was so desperate to have understanding. I wanted to know what God's calling was for me, and how I could fulfill the destiny He said I was given when I was formed in my mother's womb. I wanted to live my life for Him and not for myself anymore because living for myself was destructive. I couldn't understand how I was on this earth, and it seemed like there was nothing more than what I was living. I had some amazing things happen in the past few months, but I still didn't understand what or why I was alive. I would spend time with Bree, and it seemed like she was doing good even though I didn't see school being her focus. She had roommates who loved to party, and that was about all I saw them do. I was worried for her, but I thought this was her time to be an adult and live life the way she wanted.

I really had no understanding of prayer and just figured it was totally normal to party a lot in college. So I didn't say much about it. My focus was truly on how I could be a better me and grow to have a better future, so I could leave Bree with something when I died. I knew the way I had been living was not what I wanted. I studied the Word of God constantly and wanted to have a grasp on how I was supposed to live to please Him. I was confused, yet there were things happening that I couldn't explain. I felt like my heart was changing. I was seeing that I was different and came to a place where I didn't even want to drink. I was just so dedicated to finding answers that I couldn't see what was happening with Bree in school or with her roommates.

I had no idea she was struggling with her faith. I would talk about the Lord with her and what I was spending time doing, and she would just tell me, "That's cool, Mom." It was wild how much I wanted her to understand that there was more to life than just partying, yet that was all I had lived for a long time. It was my *normal.* I didn't even have a grasp on who I was, so how was I to be an example for her?

The year ended well, and Bree and I celebrated the Holidays with my mother in Michigan. One of her roommates even came with us. It was a good Christmas, but I still had this desire and emptiness that I didn't fully understand.

CHAPTER 3

THE ENCOUNTER

January 2018

As I was spending every minute in scripture, I began to see things clearly. I started to truly believe that I was valuable, and even as a sinner, Jesus came to save me. It wasn't just because I was this filthy sinner who made a million mistakes, but it was because I was a lost daughter. One thing that changed a lot for me was realizing that trust and forgiveness are two very separate things. I saw in scripture where the Lord said:

> **It is better to trust in the Lord than to put confidence in man. (Psalm 118:8 KJV)**

Plus:

> **And when you pray, make sure you forgive the faults of others so that your Father in heaven will also forgive you. (Matthew 6:14 TPT)**

I asked the Lord to reveal any unforgiveness, bitterness, or resentment in my heart. I began to whole heartedly ask forgiveness for Chad, Jade, my mother, and anyone I could think of who had hurt me in the past. I forgave them and proclaimed it out loud, and then I began to ask Father to forgive them as well. I felt so much healing throughout this time. I was being set free from unforgiveness and bitterness that I hadn't even realized I was holding onto. I was starting to listen to only worship music and refused to listen to anything else. I remember K-Love, a radio station, doing a challenge and stating that if you only listen to Christian music for thirty days, you will not be the same. I took that challenge seriously and found some of the most awesome music on YouTube that was actually good for my spirit.

I started spending more time with Dorothy, asking more questions and listening to her wisdom. She was a very charismatic woman, and at the time, I didn't even understand what charismatic was. Sally was also spending time with me. Sally had a different view on things. She had made some comments that threw me off like when she said she would smoke pot if it was legal. She was mentoring women and in charge of women's studies at the church, so it made me question some things. I was learning who Holy Spirit was and how we are given power and authority here on earth. We are called to be the hands and feet of Jesus. I realized the same Holy Spirit that raised Jesus from the grave actually lived inside of me and that Jesus says, "Follow Me." I started to see in the Word that the Lord calls us to heal the sick, cast out demons, and cleanse the lepers. I was starting to take His Word literally and just trust what He said above all else.

On January 17, 2018, I was alone in my travel trailer studying and seeking as I had been for months. It was so funny because I had so many moments with the Lord that actually made me giggle out loud. One time as I was reading, I saw in scripture where the Word talked about fasting. I was never taught about fasting. Actually going without food sounded crazy, but there it was, in the Word of God. So I stopped reading and said, "Lord, I want to fast for you. You're all I need." I instantly felt like He said, "You are silly. You are fasting." At that moment, I looked up at the clock, and it was a little after 6:00 p.m., and I realized I hadn't eaten all day. It was just little things like this that were happening and just blew my mind.

I have heard a few teachings on fasting and read several books. The one that really helped me better understand was, *'Fasting'* by Jentezen Franklin. He goes on to describe (page 65),

> "Fasting is a constant means of renewing yourself spiritually. The discipline of fasting breaks you out of the world's routine. It is a form of worship-offering your body to God as a living sacrifice is holy and pleasing to God (Rom. 12:1). The discipline of fasting will humble you, remind you of your dependency on God, and bring you back to your first love. It causes the roots of your relationship with Jesus to go deeper."

You can also check out, *'Fasting,'* by Michael Dow. I love when he shares this;

> "If fasting is about food and only food, then that means fasting is not about television. Fasting is not about social media. Fasting is not about entertainment. Fasting is not about the way that you spend money on certain things, or places you like to go. I understand that there is a tendency in our day to consider other things to be "fasting," but in reality these things are not truly fasting as much as they are disciplines."

He goes on to explain that fasting without prayer is just starving yourself. I love how direct Mr. Dow expresses that it is exercising self-discipline to not allow social media your time, or television, and so on; not fasting. These two books are what I would recommend to anyone that has an interest in better understanding fasting.

I told the Lord I wanted all He wanted to give me. If it was from Him, I was in. I had been seeking the gift of tongues even though at the age of fourteen, when I first heard people speaking in tongues, I literally walked out and lit a joint, thinking, *These people are crazy*. Here I was, thirty-nine years old and seeking the same thing I once thought was crazy. I asked God for all the gifts. I wanted anything and everything He wanted to give me, and I was open to receive. I read in the book of Acts that the disciples were baptized with Holy Spirit and began speaking in different tongues. Then I read in 1 Corinthians that there is a heavenly language called tongues. I understood it to be your spirit speaking to God and knowing what to say or ask even if I didn't have understanding.

When someone speaks in tongues, no one understands a word he says, because he's not speaking to people, but to God-he is speaking intimate mysteries in the Spirit. (1 Corinthians 14:2 TPT)

I may not have had full understanding, but I was seeing it was in God's Word; and above all else, I believed His Word. As the night went on, I began praying and thanking the Lord for who He is, for what He was doing, and for what He was going to do; and all of a sudden, a fire—a tangible (physical) fire—began to rise inside of my chest. I began speaking in tongues in an almost gibberish sound. I had never spoken like that before, and it was flowing out of me supernaturally, and I couldn't stop it. At that very moment, I heard this thought, "Zara, you are almost forty years old. What are you doing?" Yet at the same moment, this indescribable peace came over; and as clear as day, I heard the words:

Trust in the Lord with all your heart and lean not on your own understanding. (Proverbs 3:5 NIV)

I began crying as I continued to speak in tongues, and it was the most intense feeling I had ever experienced. My entire body began to feel fire, not a burning fire but a comforting consuming fire of peace, warmth, and love like I'd never known. I can't explain how long I continued to speak in tongues, but I remember at one point I thought I would never speak normally again, and I didn't even care. I was in the most loving arms of the creator of the universe, and I knew that what was happening to me was Holy Spirit. I believe that I can honestly say to this day that I have never felt so overwhelmed by the feeling of belonging and love as I did at that moment. It felt like God saved me and found me in my mess but came with nothing except overwhelming love. He wasn't condemning me or angry at me. He was just loving on me.

For days, I ended up lying on my couch with my Bible grasped in my arms against my chest (as if hugging His Word), and all I would say was, "I love you." It was so intense because I felt like I could hear Him say, "I love you, too," every single time. On January 20, I had a conviction and realized that I didn't want to smoke cigarettes anymore. I didn't want to take pills, drink, or smoke weed. So I literally grabbed all I had in my house and threw everything in the trash because I knew all of that had a voice to me. I ended up grabbing the bag and taking it out of the trailer. I went back inside, and I got dramatic. I grabbed my Bible and started stomping the floor, yelling, "Addiction, you no longer have authority over my life. I will not listen to you anymore. You are done telling me what to do!" I meant every word, and at that very moment, I was delivered of everything.

The fire I felt lasted for a couple of weeks. I ran to my daughter and my little brother to tell them what had happened, and they both thought I had lost my mind. Yet I had finally found it. I had zero cravings for cigarettes after being a smoker for over twenty years. I had no desire to drink or anything else. It was amazing. Dakota tried to tell me it was all in my mind, but I knew this was way bigger than something I just imagined. I knew me, and I knew the time I had given to God and the prayers I was saying in my secret place all alone with no one watching or listening.

Soon after this happened, the Lord would wake me up at 3:00 a.m. (which lasted for about a month), and I would just pray for Dorothy. I didn't understand why, but I didn't ask questions. My prayer life was completely changing.

I realized most of my prayers were all about God doing something for me rather than thanking Him for being with me. I began believing, without any doubt, that there was so much more to this than I had ever imagined. God is real, He is alive, and He simply wants a relationship with us. Jesus clearly tells the woman at the well;

> **Yet a time is coming and has now come when the true worshipers will worship the Father in the Spirit and in truth, for they are the kind of worshipers the Father seeks. God is spirit, and his worshipers must worship in Spirit and in truth. (John 4:23–24 NIV)**

What is He saying? He is saying that the Lord wants worship from our hearts and minds—real worship, real relationship. He wants us to choose Him, and He is such a good, good Father that He will not force us to choose Him. He will never take away our free will. I believe that when we rely on everyone else to teach us about Him and don't spend time alone seeking Him, we can get so lost. Most of us will end up offended or angry and even walk away from God because of another's behavior. We seriously have to ask ourselves though, Is our faith in the preacher/teacher/people, or is our faith in God? Some of the meanest people I've met were in church, but their behavior and judgment are not who Jesus is. Our Father doesn't treat us anywhere near the way we tend to treat one another.

Most of us will spend hours in front of our televisions, but we won't spend thirty minutes in the Bible. I used to think that the King James translation was the only version that was the truth. Yet as time has gone by and I have spent time in scripture, I confess I love all the translations. It amazes me when someone says, "It's just a man-written book that's been translated millions of times." I can't really help but laugh a little. If we serve a mighty God that we believe split the Red Sea, defeated death, and was raised from the grave, why do we not believe that He has the power to protect His Word? Plus, the Bible doesn't contain God; it reveals Him, and we find who we are through Him.

Now I study with about four translations; The Passion Translation being one of my favorites because of the heart it reveals. It just speaks the passion of Father's heart so beautifully in my opinion. But I love my King James, my New International, my Message translation, and many others. They are all saying the same things in different ways. It is beautiful because scripture actually says that Holy Spirit is our guide, teacher, and comforter (see John 14:26). This means that we can always turn to Father and ask for answers. He states that His children receive not because they ask not.

> **You want what you don't have, so you scheme and kill to get it. You are jealous of what others have, but you can't get it, so you fight and wage war to take it away from them. Yet you don't have what you want because you don't ask God for it. And even when you ask, you don't get it because your motives are all wrong-you want only what will give you pleasure. (James 4:2–3 NLT)**

By the end of January, I was so on fire that I was beyond zealous. Bree had come to me and explained that she could see I was so different. Even my language changed, and I didn't use swear words anymore. That was not from me trying not to cuss. I assure you; it just happened. She told me she was struggling, and her roommates had ordered a satanic bible, and she didn't want to be there anymore. I told her it was okay, and college would always be there. If she wanted to come home, she could, and she did. Although being around me was annoying to her, I couldn't watch television anymore; it just wasn't for me. All I wanted to talk about was the Lord and His Word. I cried a lot and just loved on her, but she didn't understand; she only knew that something happened to me, and it had changed me. She didn't like going places with me much either because I couldn't contain myself. I would walk through Walmart or any store and just tell people that Jesus loved them like everyone I saw. I was a changed woman, and I didn't know how to handle what was happening to me as well.

Then things really took a wild turn for me. To this day, I have a hard time explaining exactly what happened, but for about three weeks, I was deafened. I know it sounds ridiculous, but I couldn't hear people when they were speaking to me. All I could hear was God and this pastor on YouTube named Dan Mohler. I began watching *School of Kingdom Living* with Dan Mohler, and everything changed. I began understanding even more that I had value and that God created me to shine His light here on earth and to live as Jesus lived.

Jesus was our example of how a true believer is supposed to live. It doesn't mean we are required to live in perfection. It means we live by grace and are unashamed. We do not need to fear the darkness. My family thought I lost my mind before, but when I was deafened, they really thought I was losing it. Yet truth is, I was truly finding my way, and God's hand was on me the entire time.

Bree ended up getting a job at an Applebee's restaurant as a hostess, and I was continuing with my studies. I started making a few videos for Facebook, just trying to share what was happening to me. I wanted to share how much God truly loves us and how He was changing my life. I wasn't sure how others would receive me, but I knew I couldn't hide all that was happening. I have never been a shy woman anyway, but the support I received shocked me. Some were so receiving and overwhelmed by my testimony of speaking in tongues; others just weren't sure if I was being for real or not. I was definitely being for real about everything and very transparent. I was even told to "slow down and enjoy the fire while it lasted" and was told other negative things as if it would all come to a stop eventually. However, I knew that nothing would ever be the same.

CHAPTER 4

THE ADVENTURE

February 2018

With all the changes happening to me, I felt like I needed to share my story with others as often as I could. I was invited to speak at another women's event that was scheduled for March 10 and was called to a meeting to discuss the upcoming event. As I sat with all the leaders of this event, I couldn't hear what was being said. My ears were plugged by God, and I could barely hear a thing. I remember later Dorothy shared with me that Sally asked her if I was okay. Dorothy knew what had happened to me and looked right into Sally's eyes and said, "Oh, she is really good." Dorothy knew that what was happening to me was all the Lord because I had reached out to her several times to share.

The meeting was good even though I didn't hear everything. There was one woman there who I got these strange feelings when she would speak or was near me. I couldn't hear well, but I knew that when she spoke, something in my spirit shifted as if a red flag or warning. I didn't understand that at all, but I dismissed it because so much was happening that I didn't think much of it. The women decided that I should be the first speaker because I was so on fire and could get the room lit up with my testimony. So it was decided and scheduled.

Bree was beginning to see that what was happening to me was real. Her faith was coming alive again, and she was starting to see that Jesus had truly done something to me. I decided to get baptized because I had a full understanding now of what it meant. It is so important to our walk with the Lord. He tells us all through the New Testament that it is so much more than just a dip in the water, a sprinkle, or a symbol. It is literally dying with Christ and then rising with Christ. It is putting the old man to death and rising up as a child of God. It is a full immersion into the grave and coming out of the water alive. Even Jesus went fully into the water. How could He have come out if He hadn't gone in? (See Matthew 3:16). The world was even baptized in Noah's time.

In the book of Acts and in many other scriptures, we see so clearly that we are called to repent and be baptized. I had gone through baptism as a child, but it was because my older brother did it, and I just thought he was the coolest person alive and always tried to do what he did. Now at this time, it was a heart cry, and I knew that it was time to fully dedicate my life to Jesus Christ. Bree decided she wanted to be baptized as well, and so we went to a church and set everything up. It was beautiful to be baptized with my daughter. I was humbled in the moment of it all.

I had attended a Baptist church for most of my life, but I never heard anyone speak in tongues or speak on the gifts of Holy Spirit, so I decided to attend a different church a friend had invited me to. It was a Pentecostal church, and they spoke in tongues, danced, and did all kinds of things I had never been exposed to in church before. I was excited to think that there were others who would understand what was happening to me.

After Bree and I were baptized, the pastor and his wife asked to meet with me. In the meeting, the pastor went on to tell me that because I was a single woman, I now needed a covering, and he and his wife would be that for me. I asked them what that meant. He went on to explain that I needed to be held accountable because I didn't have a husband, and they were there to fill that role. I was so confused by what he said, but I didn't argue because

I didn't know if it was true or not. I just wanted to be obedient and follow whatever the Lord wanted me to do.

As soon as I got home, I sat down on my couch and asked the Lord to please speak to me and show me what the pastor and his wife were talking about. I instantly felt peace and knew that Jesus Christ was my covering, and my accountability was in the hands of my Father. I had a relationship with the creator of the universe, why would I allow someone to tell me what I could and could not do? I was being obedient to the Lord and wanted to do nothing short of being pleasing to God. I didn't understand why they would tell me that, but I knew whose hands my life was in, and I knew what God had done inside of me. I was not a lost woman anymore. I was a found daughter to the Highest King. It is my job to steward the motives of my heart:

> **Keep thy heart with all diligence; for out of it are the issues of life. (Proverbs 4:23 KJV)**

At the time, being so new to a church and not knowing anyone well, I was really unsure and didn't have an understanding of what the pastor and his wife were trying to share with me. I still don't fully agree with the way I was approached, but I do have a better understanding that it is good to be surrounded by people who will pray for you and with you. At first, it felt like they were trying to take authority over me, and to be honest, that wasn't working for me at all. I was so on fire for Jesus I didn't need anyone to tell me that I had to answer to them or be held accountable to them. They didn't even know me personally or explain with a heart to help. At least it didn't feel that way to me. I never did go back to that church, but I loved everyone there and am still connected with a few of its members.

> **But the wonderful anointing you have received from God is so much greater than their deception and now lives in you. There's no need for anyone to keep teaching you.**

> **His anointing teaches you all that you need to know, for it will lead you into truth, not a counterfeit. So just as the anointing has taught you, remain in him.(1 John 2:27 TPT)**

I started having friends that didn't understand what was happening to me, telling me I was more fun when I was drinking. My brother made fun of me a lot during this time as well. Every time I went into the store with my daughter, she would literally go the other way and tell me to text her when I was ready. I wasn't embarrassed by their reactions toward me. I knew I was different. All I could say was, "Jesus changed everything."

I began researching Dan Mohler and where he would be speaking because I knew I had to meet him. I had a list of questions, and I figured that since I could hear him clearly, he would be the right person to ask. I found an event he was scheduled to speak at in Middlebury, Indiana, and I made arrangements to attend. I wanted my mother to go with me and Bree to go as well. So every one of us got things planned and scheduled to attend the event.

Bree was staying at her best friend's house a lot. She just wasn't sure of me, but she loved me, and that never changed. There was a week that I don't share with many people. After the physical fire, which my family could even feel come off of my body, began to fade, I began to start questioning everything that had happened. Was it real? Did God really set me free? Was this experience real? I spent about five days sitting still on the living room floor of my travel trailer just questioning everything. I had the worst thoughts about killing myself, going to get a bottle of alcohol, and going to get cigarettes—just smoke a joint Zara.

I kept hearing the words some of my friends had said with regard to how much fun I used to be when I drank. It was crazy. I had just experienced something I had never imagined, and for five days, I was thinking of things that weren't even in my heart. I asked Sally to come pray for me and explained what was happening. She shared with me some of her experiences with deliverances and things like that. So I thought she was the best person to reach out to.

I didn't fully understand deliverance or what that looked like. I knew my Bible talked a lot about freedom in Christ, and I believed that with my entire heart. I knew I had been set free from things I never imagined possible and even things I didn't realize until years later. At this weak point, I was having thoughts that I didn't understand and didn't know what else to do. Sally ended up coming to my house and praying over me and my home. She anointed my door and windows with oil and said prayers that I had never heard anyone say before. She was commanding the devil to leave and proclaiming victory over me. It was wild at certain points because I didn't know how to react, but what I did see was a woman who believed what she was praying. I did see a woman who was fighting for me, and I felt her love for me. The thoughts didn't stop until a few days later when I decided I wasn't going to sit there and take it anymore.

I finally stood up and yelled out loud, "I am not going backward. I am not giving into drinking or going to get cigarettes. I am not the woman I used to be. I am a citizen of heaven. I am a child of the King. I belong to God, and I will not sit here and listen to this anymore." It was at that moment that all those thoughts stopped. It was wild, but I didn't think about any of those things again and began studying the Word of God again and was actually able to focus. I was finally free after days of torment. I didn't fully understand until later that all I needed to do was take my authority and proclaim truth over myself.

My niece was allowed to come over often before I had this encounter. Soon after it, though, my brother's girlfriend couldn't even look at me. She hated that I had given my life to Jesus and would try to tell me she didn't understand. She would say things like, "Will you pray that I will quit drinking? But I still want to smoke pot." I had no idea how to respond to some of the things she was saying. It was wild that she literally wasn't able to look at me either. Her eyes seemed so dark, and she just didn't want to hear anything about scripture or the things I was experiencing.

When my brother's girlfriend would ask me certain questions, I would just answer honestly and explain that I didn't know the answer. One question a friend asked me was, "Why does God let babies die if He's so good?" That I knew was a pretty easy answer because there is an enemy that comes to kill, steal, and destroy. That answer never satisfies most people though because they want someone to blame, and if it's not God, they just don't feel justified in their anger.

On February 16, 2018, Bree came home from work and was hurting so bad that she couldn't step up into the travel trailer. I ended up lifting her and helping to get her in. It just so happened that I was growing in understanding that Jesus is the same yesterday, today, and forever. I heard some testimonies about healing and the power of stepping into faith. I read this scripture earlier that was speaking to my heart:

> **He told them, "It was because of your lack of faith. I promise you, if you have faith inside of you no bigger than the size of a small mustard seed, you can say to this mountain, 'Move away from here and go over there,' and you will see it move! There is nothing you couldn't do!" (Matthew 17:20 TPT)**

I realized that most of the time, I was taking my mountains to God while He is saying He has given us the authority to tell the mountains to move, and they will move. The scripture goes on to explain that the kind of unbelief the disciples had only come out through prayer and fasting. God's Word is truly amazing. I was shocked when I started really reading and believing what His Word says.

As I helped Bree to the chair, and she sat down, I asked her if it would be okay if I just prayed for her really quick. She kind of rolled her eyes, but she said, "Sure." What happened next is another reason I am where I am today. All I did was grab her feet and said this simple prayer, "In the name of Jesus Christ, I command this pain to leave right now!" I looked at Bree and said, "Okay, now stand up and tell me what you feel." When she stood up, her eyes looked about to pop out of her head. She literally couldn't believe it, and honestly, it was like a fire started in me all over again. She said all the pain was gone, and I just jumped up and down asking if anything else hurt. Oh, my, now what do you do with me?

That was it for me. I told Bree we had to go to town. There were more people there I could pray for. I was so excited that I could barely contain myself. Bree and I were supposed to go see her friend who worked at Taco Bell, so we headed there first. It was so much fun. Bree talked to her friend while I talked to the young girl at the cash register. I asked her if anything hurt, and she said her knees were giving her problems. So I asked her to step out from behind the counter and let me pray for her real quick, and she did.

After I prayed, the girl tested her knees out and was freaked out because the pain was gone. My mind was so blown, but I knew God was good, and I couldn't deny He can do anything. Just look at what He did to me, so how could I deny it? We ended up heading to Walmart, and this time, Bree didn't leave me when we walked in. She actually walked with me.

We went straight to the back of the store, and there was a young man selling cable in front of the electronics department. As we approached him, I could feel something off, but we walked up, and I told him he was loved and valuable. He looked at me like I was loony, but yet when I asked him if I could pray for him, he started crying and said yes. He told Bree and I that he suffered from depression and anxiety and could definitely use some prayer. So that was exactly what we did. We prayed for him together. It was amazing. There, my daughter was praying with me and not so embarrassed.

When we left Walmart, we went to pick up Bree's friend who was out of work now from Taco Bell. On the way home, she complained that she had burned herself at work, and it was a fresh burn that hurt really bad. So me being me, I said, "Girl, let me pray for you. God is good, and He loves you." She placed her arm forward, and I prayed for healing and for the pain to leave. She then freaked out. It didn't hurt anymore, and she was shocked. It was so exciting that I went home, and with her permission, we made a quick video with the testimony of what happened. At this time, my hearing wasn't back 100 percent, but it was starting to get clearer. I was able to hear a lot better than I had been.

I will give you the keys of heaven's kingdom realm to forbid on earth that which is forbidden in heaven, and to release on earth that which is released in heaven. (Matthew 16:19 TPT)

As soon as we were done making the testimony video, I ran next door to my friend's uncle. I ran inside his house and threw my coat on the floor. He was sitting in his recliner, and I just blurted out, "God is going to heal your knees. Right now."

As I write this, I recall how excited I was. My friend just looked at me with a blank face and said, "Okay." See, my friend had no cartilage in either of his knees, and the doctors had been telling him for years that they wanted to give him knee replacement.

When I walked over to him, I placed my hands on both knees and said, "Lord, you are the God of the impossible. I am asking for a miracle right now. Cartilage, grow in Jesus name." As soon as I said that, there was the most incredible feeling under my hands. It was as if the Lord was rebuilding his knees. Within forty-five minutes, my friend was bending his knees and able to climb stairs like he had brand-new knees. At that point, all of my dreams and focus changed. I no longer cared about my book, my motivational speaking events, nothing. I just wanted to live the rest of my life following Jesus.

I had no idea what to do. You think if something like that was going to happen, there would be smoke filling the room and some angelic music playing supernaturally or something, but it was so simple and so natural. The supernatural really should be our natural when we follow Jesus Christ. My friend continued testing his knees, and it was finished—he was healed.

To this day, I will get a random text from him about once a year saying his knees are still good. That was it. I went home and laid down. As I stared at my hands, I asked the Lord to never allow me to forget what that felt like. That was the very first day I began praying for others. I was not the same woman after I had such a massive encounter with Holy Spirit, but that night, everything I ever thought I knew meant nothing. My life was and has been forever changed. Oh, just wait. This testimony gets even wilder.

I began praying for people everywhere I went. I was beginning to witness some of the most amazing things. One time, in Walmart, I was walking and saw a woman in a motorized wheelchair. Of course, I asked her what in the world was she doing in that wheelchair because she looked so young. She explained she had fibromyalgia, was dehydrated, felt weak, and simply couldn't walk right. I asked her if I could pray for her, and her husband instantly rolled his eyes, but she said yes. So I laid my hand on her shoulder and began praying for her. It was so intense as Holy Spirit began touching her. I finished praying and asked her to please stand up and see if she felt better.

As tears began to roll down her face, she stood up and looked at her husband. She said she literally felt like she was almost floating, and she felt warmth all over as I was praying for her. She said she felt so much better. Still rolling his eyes, the husband just stood there with his arms crossed across his chest. She was so filled up with light that she even refused to get back in the wheelchair. I told her that I truly bless her and wished them the best as I began to walk away.

I felt in my Spirit that the Lord said, "You're not done." As I walked back out of the aisle that I had gone in, the couple was still standing in the same spot. The man's arms were still crossed, and the woman was still trying to convince him what she felt was real.

I walked back up to the couple and asked if they knew Jesus or had a relationship with Him. The woman wept as she began to explain, "You don't understand. We just lost our son, and things are not right." My heart instantly felt the weight of their pain, and all I could do was apologize for their loss. I then asked if I could pray for both of them, and even though the man still had his arms crossed, he agreed, as well as the woman.

I placed my hands, one on each of their shoulders, and I began to pray. I said something along these lines, "Lord, we come to you humbly and open to your healing. Father, I ask that you bless this mother and father. I ask that you touch their hearts and remind them that it is not you who comes to kill, steal, or destroy. I ask that you remind them that this life is so short, and blaming you will not heal their pain. That when holidays come, they pull together and are able to remember all of the good moments they were blessed with, with their child. That the enemy doesn't divide them but that you pull them together with the unconditional love you have for them."

When I opened my eyes, the man's arms were down by his side, and he was weeping. The couple came together and embraced each other as they cried and kept telling me, "Thank you. Thank you so much." I reminded them that they were valuable to Father and that they would be okay. I encouraged them that God only wants a relationship with them and wants them to seek Him, and they would find Him. The man was so intense, and after the prayer, he was so open and fragile.

It was beautiful to see God love on them and give them some peace in the worst moment of their lives. I walked away with my mind blown and my heart overwhelmed. I simply kept praising the Lord and telling Him thank you for allowing me to be a part of His plan. I continued to stay in His Word and would share some of the testimonies on Facebook through video, but I always shared with my brother and daughter. I don't think they knew what to say. Honestly, each day was a new adventure for me, and I had no idea what to expect.

I decided to do a fast before meeting with Pastor Dan Mohler and headed up to my mother in Michigan. When my daughter and I got there, I explained that I wasn't joining them for dinner. My mother really started showing that she didn't understand. She had been challenging everything that was happening to me already, but now it was way worse. She asked me questions like, "What makes you think the Bible is real when all the other religions believe just as much in their gods?" and many other things that I simply couldn't answer in a way she understood. I wasn't praying for people in the name of Buddha or any other deity. I believed my Bible. I believe Jesus died on the cross because I am a sinner but also because I was a lost daughter. I believe He defeated death and resurrected three days later. I don't believe in or follow any other belief, so all I knew to say was, "I just believe in Jesus, Mom."

My mother was so challenged with all that was happening to me that she started reading her Bible to use scripture against me. She didn't have an understanding of most of the scripture she was using and was simply verse-plucking to make herself sound like she was right. I didn't feel like it was a competition, but she began treating my encounter as if she had to show that she knew more about God's Word. Yet with each thing she would say, she would just sound like she was attacking my testimony and everything I was experiencing.

Now my mother had been diagnosed with fibromyalgia, and she took a lot of pain pills. That was where I would get my pain pills because she would share. I told her that I believed that she would be healed at this event and to come with the expectation that God was going to do something big. I had been seeing way too much to have any doubt at that time.

On the day of the event, I walked into the church with my mother and daughter and was so excited I could barely stand it. As soon as I walked in, I started sharing with anyone who would listen to me. I was at a table with some folks when I heard these two women say, "Is that her? That sounds like her." As they approached me, they were both filled with joy and had huge smiles on their faces. They explained to me that they had been following my journey on Facebook and knew it was me the moment they heard my voice. It was such a huge shock to me because it encouraged my heart to know that by me sharing my testimony, others were being encouraged. I connected with the ladies, and we exchanged our information and are still connected to this day.

Once the event started, I was overwhelmed with the Lord's presence. Pastor Mohler looked a little different up close but ministered such a good message; it was amazing. In the end, he asked if anyone needed healing in their bodies, and people all over the sanctuary began raising their hands. He then asked anyone, with faith, to find someone with their hands raised and to lay their hands on them. So we did. My mother raised her hand, and my daughter instantly put her hand on my mom's shoulder. Pastor Dan then led us through prayer, and when he was done, he asked those who were seeking healing to check their bodies. Several people were healed, and my mother began lifting her arms above her head and was completely shocked. She was healed and in no more pain, which she hadn't experienced in a long time. It was the most awesome moment. Plus, my daughter was the one God used, and it was beyond exciting for my heart. It also encouraged Bree tremendously.

Once the event was over, I had a list of questions in my pocket for Pastor Mohler and ended up waiting until the very last person was done talking to him. We waited for hours because the line was so long, but it was worth the wait. I pulled out the list, and Pastor Dan laughed and said something about me not playing around. We sat down and talked for quite a while. My mother just sat back and said nothing. Later, she told me that she didn't want to interrupt our conversation, but it was strange to me since she had so many questions earlier in the day. I asked questions about prayer, belief, how to respond to others, and so much more. He was so kind to give me his time and answered every question I had. He kept looking at Bree and told her that God had huge plans for her. She would just look down and say thank you each time he spoke to her. We ended up leaving, and my mother came back to Indiana with us to spend time with my brother, his girlfriend, and their baby girl.

When it was time to take my mother back to her home in Michigan, my mother, Bree, and I stopped by Denny's restaurant to eat. As we were ordering our food, I felt like the Lord was telling me that our waitress had issues with her back and knee. I can't explain how I knew, but it is almost like an impression pressing on my heart. Sometimes, I will physically feel pain for a moment and know that it isn't me, so I ask others around me if they are hurting where I am feeling the pain. Honestly, nine out of ten times, that is the case and someone will speak up.

I began sharing the gospel and what Jesus was doing in my life with the waitress, and she began crying. I asked her if we could pray for her, and she said yes. She said to give her just a few minutes so she could sit down with us. Once she walked away, I looked at Bree and said, "I'm sorry. I know when I do this it embarrasses you, sweetheart."

At that moment, Bree replied by saying, "It's okay, Mom. I'm used to it, and it doesn't really bother me anymore."

I couldn't begin to express how much those words meant to me. My daughter was accepting me the way I am, and even though everything happened so fast to me, she was beginning to see it wasn't me trying to change. Jesus was and is changing everything in me. Through my surrender, He was and is able to use me in the most amazing ways because I came to realize my life is not my own. I wasn't placed here to live for myself. I am here to bring glory to Him. He calls us to be the light in the midst of the darkness and to not walk around with a basket on our heads.

> **Your lives light up the world. For how can you hide a city that stands on a hilltop? And who would light a lamp and then hide it in an obscure place? Instead, it's placed where everyone in the house can benefit from its light. So don't hide your light! Let it shine brightly before others, so that your commendable works will shine as light upon them, and then they will give their praise to your Father in heaven. (Matthew 5:14–16 TPT)**

After a few minutes, the waitress came over and sat down next to me. She began to explain that she had issues with her back and knee and then went on to share her heart on some things she was struggling with. I shared a little more with her and then asked if it was okay if I place my hand on her. I always ask permission before touching someone. She agreed, and we all began to pray for her. By the end, she was crying and said she could feel warmth all throughout her body. Her pain had left her, and she was overwhelmed by the presence of Holy Spirit. It was another moment that was just huge, and inside, I was doing jumping jacks. I had such a hard time containing my excitement every time I would pray for someone and Father would move in that moment. How or what do you do with that?

Bree and I took my mother home, and while there, I saw that there was an event in Texas called "Power and Love." It was with a preacher named Todd White, but I was more interested in his guest speaker, Heidi Baker. I had started listening and seeing so many ministers online who were walking out the things I was experiencing. By this time, my ears were opened, and I could hear people around me. I was so hungry to grow in the Lord and understand all that I was experiencing.

I found something called Pioneer School with Torben Sondergaard and also began watching Bill Johnson, Shawn Bolz, Randy Clark, Robby Dawkins, and so many others. I was fascinated with their lives and what they were preaching. I was thrown off by some of the things they said, but I saw in scripture where so much of what they said was right there in the Word of God. I had no idea about the "Christianese" language and was hearing words I had never heard before. Yes, the charismatic has an entirely different language and words. There are times, to this day, I really wish I hadn't learned all of that stuff, but here I am, aware and knowing.

The first time I saw Heidi Baker online, I was so drawn in by her behavior and what was happening in her life. This woman's testimony shocked me, and I wanted to talk to her to ask some questions. I would try to look away from her on the screen of my old laptop, but I couldn't. She was so different and unique. I had never seen someone sit on a church stage and just cry out to the Lord the way she did. I instantly felt like the Lord said to buy a ticket, and although I didn't have very much money, I pushed the button to purchase. There I was with a ticket to a conference all the way in Texas set for April. I had no idea how I would get there or even where I would stay. I decided that if I had to hitchhike, so be it. I would be there no matter what.

CHAPTER 5

THE SIGNS AND WONDERS

March 2018

Bree and I stayed at my mother's for a few days because we had tickets to a TobyMac concert and were excited to go worship in an arena full of other believers. As we drove away from my mother's house, I felt like the Lord said, "There are drugs in your truck." Not understanding what in the world that would mean, I ignored the warning. By this time, I didn't smoke pot or cigarettes. I was completely sober for the first time in over twenty years. I didn't even have the desire, so I knew that there was no way there were drugs in my truck.

Bree and I enjoyed the concert although I cried like a baby most of the time. I was shocked that people just sat in their seats and weren't standing, lifting their arms, and just giving God all the praise. I was so fresh in my walk with the Lord. I didn't understand at the time, but there is such a huge difference between a concert and a worship night.

At one point, while I was crying and saying, "They just don't understand how much He loves us," my daughter stood up with me and said, "I'll stand with you, Mom." It just made me cry even more. I was so overwhelmed by God's goodness I didn't understand how others were not. Bree and I left that concert closer and more connected than we had been in a long time. I think she thought I was a bit over the top, but my heart was pure, and I didn't want to play a Christian; I wanted to do nothing but live for Jesus.

Bree and I got home pretty late that night, and we crashed as soon as we hit our beds. At the time, I gave Bree the only bed in my travel trailer, and I slept on the couch. We didn't have much for a long time, but we were thankful to have each other.

Dorothy and I were becoming closer in our friendship. I would always call her or go to her house to share testimonies of what God was doing when I would go to the stores. She ended up wanting to go with me, and when she did, that was it. She told me she wanted to go to the store any time I would. It was so funny because she told me, "Zara, if you go anywhere, you better come get me." She was seeing what was happening, and she was excited to be a part of it. We grew such a love for each other. I had never understood what it was to have a sister in Christ until Dorothy. She encouraged me, prayed with me, prayed for my daughter, and continued to pour her wisdom into me. I praise the Lord that He brought Dorothy and me together even now.

When I woke up the next morning, I jumped in my truck and headed toward town. Again, I heard, "There are drugs in your truck." I looked back and saw the black bag my mother had sent for my brother and instantly stopped the truck. I wasn't going to ignore this again. I walked to the back door, opened it, and ripped the bag that had a blanket in it, and there it was. There were about three or four containers of prescription fentanyl that had belonged to my uncle Carl. I couldn't believe it. I was so angry that it almost brought me to tears. I turned my truck around and called Dakota. I told him if he didn't come get this crap, I was going to throw it all in the burn pile. Then I called my mother. She was mad at me for being mad; it was absurd. I ended up crying and just hung up the phone. My family didn't understand I was not playing. My life was not the same, and things that didn't bother me before were now breaking my heart.

Instead of hurting because of others, I began hurting for others. My heart was so broken by the decisions my family was making, and I knew the only reason they made fun of me was just their ignorance of the truth of Jesus Christ and His love for us. I can't explain why my mother thought it was okay to sneak drugs into my truck, but I gave God praise that my daughter and I weren't pulled over or caught with those things. I was so upset by the entire thing, and my brother came right out and took them. My heart didn't know how to handle what happened, and I ended up heading to Dorothy to ask for her advice and prayer.

She was always there for me. She had an open heart, and her story was so cool. She was kicked out of the Baptist church over twenty years prior, she and like seven others, because they began speaking in tongues, and the church claimed they were a distraction and causing division in the congregation. That always blew me away because she was the sweetest woman I had ever known.

At the end of the month, we celebrated my niece's birthday, and it was fun. It was funny to me how everyone I knew would listen to me share but would look at me like I had lost my mind. I was never called a liar because those I shared with knew I didn't lie. They just didn't know how to take me and the things I was sharing. I was madly in love with Jesus, and I was on fire for Him. My life didn't look anything like it used too. I was not sure those who knew me had any idea what to do with me. I was thankful to be alive, and I wasn't wasting any more time on things of this world.

> **Do not love the world or anything in the world. If anyone loves the world, love for the Father is not in them. For everything in the world-the lust of the flesh, the lust of the eyes, and the pride of life-comes not from the Father but from the world. The world and its desires pass away, but whoever does the will of God lives forever. (1 John 2:15–17 NIV)**

On March 7, 2018, there was a local church holding what they called a "revival." I talked Bree into going with me to check it out. By this time, she was way more open to talking about the Lord with me, and she was okay with the life I was living. She still made fun of me at times, but she didn't hesitate to come to me when she needed prayer.

I remember one night she had a nightmare and woke me up to pray for her. She slept well the rest of the night. I was thankful for the little openness she had and was positive she would encounter Holy Spirit one day, perhaps the way I had. When we attended the revival, the preacher asked if anyone suffered from depression, and Bree stood up. I admit. I didn't realize she was dealing with depression, but I was thankful that she was seeking freedom. After the preacher said a prayer, Bree looked at me and said, "Something is different, Mom. It's like a weight came off of me when he prayed." I didn't know what to do except to thank the Lord for His goodness and for delivering Bree from that bondage.

On March 10, the ladies' church event was all set to go forward with me being the first speaker. I wasn't nervous at all. I have never had trouble speaking in front of people, and now it was to share all God was doing in my life. I had nothing to rehearse or practice because all I had to do was share the truth of what I was seeing and experiencing. I was honestly excited to share, and now it was in front of women who came to hear and not just random people I was stopping in the store.

I remember the ordained minister who was our main speaker came up to me and said, "Zara, the one piece of advice I would like to give you is to keep going. Don't let anyone convince you that you have to have some certificate to preach the Gospel. Jesus has already given you the green light. You are certified because of your testimony because you are His." That has stuck with me throughout all these years.

The women began coming into the church and finding their seats. I recall my spirit doing those jumping jacks with excitement. There were so many times I didn't know what I was going to say to people, but somehow, the words would just come.

> **When you are brought before synagogues, rulers and authorities, do not worry about how you will defend yourself or what you will say,**

for the Holy Spirit will teach you at that time what you should say. (Luke 12:11–12 NIV)

The event began, and I took my place at the pulpit. I started sharing who I was and what had happened to me throughout the past couple of months. I shared how I was lit on fire by the power of Holy Spirit and how I realized that the same Spirit that raised Jesus from the grave now lived inside of me and how I was set free from all of my addictions. I shared the healing testimonies I was witnessing and how I was deafened for a short time. It was incredible the way that the room was filled with the presence of God. Most of the women were so excited with me, and others weren't sure because here stood a tattooed woman claiming that Jesus loved us so very much. Some people can't see past my tattoos, but God does. He loves me and my tattoos. When others use the scripture found in Leviticus about not marking our bodies, it truly shocks me why they would try to manipulate the Word of God.

In those times, people were branding and marking their bodies unto other gods. That was unacceptable to the Lord and still is. When people would call out my tattoos, I would just simply reply that my body is the temple of Holy Spirit, and I have never been in a church that wasn't decorated. We are the church, not a building.

As a believer of Jesus Christ, we are now His body—His church here on earth. Not many have a response to that, but I am not here to debate someone's theology. All I know is what happened to me and that I am no longer an orphan but a child of God, and I am loved by Him whether I am loved by others or not. I am accepted by God, and that means if someone doesn't accept me, it's okay because I am already accepted, and I don't live to please people but to be pleasing to my Father.

Now we're no longer living like slaves under the law, but we enjoy being God's very own sons and daughters! And because we're his, we can access everything our Father has—for

we are heirs because of what God has done! (Galatians 4:7 TPT)

Am I now trying to win the approval of human beings, or of God? Or am I trying to please people? If I were still trying to please people, I would not be a servant of Christ. (Galatians 1:10 NIV)

The event was amazing with several wonderful and beautiful sisters in Christ speaking. The woman who had made my spirit shift during our previous meeting began to sing her song, and the entire atmosphere shifted. It was off, and I didn't have a full understanding of it at all. I asked Sally, who was in charge, if she felt the shift. She just looked at me and said, "Yes, I feel it. I know, Zara." With not having understanding, I just sat back and knew that this was not of God.

Once the woman was done and the next speaker began, the atmosphere in the sanctuary shifted again, and there was peace. I knew enough to know that the woman should have never been allowed a microphone or any authority over that event, but I didn't know enough to understand why Sally allowed it when she was aware of everything. As the atmosphere shifted, the Lord began moving in mighty ways. In the end, there were several women who received their prayer language, and several others were healed from back issues and more. One woman even removed her oxygen and proclaimed she was healed and could breathe just fine again. It was something you just would have had to see to believe, yet that is the opposite of our faith. We walk by faith and not by sight. God does some amazing things when we just trust Him.

After the event, I began receiving messages and calls from random people asking me to come pray for them. One friend messaged me about her daughter and asked if I would come and lay hands on her because she was suffering from a migraine. Without hesitation, I went straight away to their home, and sure enough, when I left, the young lady was healed and no longer suffering.

I can't begin to explain how or why, but all I know is that these things began to change my entire life, and all of my focus was on my Father. I was surrendered to whatever He wanted, and I didn't want to do anything else but talk about Him and His love for us. Soon after, somehow, I began mentoring women who would meet me in the local coffee shop, and I would just minister about identity and who God says we are as His children. I just loved being His and walked out whatever He called me to do.

I'll never forget speaking with one woman who asked me about a prostitute in scripture. I had no idea what she was talking about. All of a sudden, I heard the word *Hosea*, and I instantly said, "Let's look in Hosea." I had no clue about the book of Hosea as I had never read it, but there it was. The story of the prophet who married the prostitute. I would be so blown away every time these things happened, and they happened a lot.

I can't express how much it felt like. I was growing and learning as I was speaking with others. I would say things, and inside, I would think, *Oh, my goodness. I didn't even know that.* It was like the Lord was teaching me while using me to teach others. It was so overwhelming, and my heart was so full. I would use the word *unbelievable* if I wasn't the one who experienced it.

Dorothy and I began having some of the most fun adventures together. She was so supportive of all the changes the Lord was doing with me and for me. There was one time we went to our local Applebee's, and the Lord moved in such indescribable ways. Dorothy and I were sitting down next to the hostess station, and we were talking and sharing some stories. I was teasing her because she was talking about her friend who absolutely loved animals, and I said something like, "I love to eat them."

She was laughing so hard and just shook her head at me. As we were sitting there, I heard the hostess say that her feet were killing her, and I just looked right at her and said, "Hey, your feet hurt?"

She said, "Yes."

I reached my hand out to her and said, "This is cool. Just give me your hand."

Without hesitation, she placed her hand in mine.

I said, "In Jesus name, pain, leave her feet right now."

As soon as I let go of her hand, her eyes got huge, and she didn't know what to say. I asked her if they still hurt, and she shook her head no. It was out of this world.

Then I heard a voice behind me say, "Wait a minute. Can you do that for me?"

I turned to see the other host who the girl had been speaking to before I had politely interrupted. He was about seventeen years old, and I asked, "What's wrong with you?"

He replied that his feet hurt too. I explained that I believed Jesus is the same yesterday, today, and forever, so yes, I would pray for him as well. It wasn't like he came up to me all perfect and ready for some spiritual encounter. We were literally just sitting in the restaurant getting ready to eat. So I asked for the young man's hand and said the same prayer and then asked him how his feet felt. This young man was so overwhelmed he began freaking out, saying, "No way. No WAY!" The pain was gone, and he simply couldn't wrap his head around what happened.

It was so funny because the next thing we knew, Dorothy and I saw him stomping around the entire restaurant. At one point, I looked up and saw him standing at the kitchen door with the cook, just pointing at me while he shared what had happened.

Then it got really exciting because as Dorothy and I were speaking with our waitress, I felt the impression that she had a Bible but didn't read it because she didn't understand it. So, me being shy and all, I ended up asking her if that was true, and her jaw about dropped to the floor. She said that she had a King James Version next to her bed, and she wanted to read it, but it just didn't make sense to her. I just encouraged her to grab a New International Version or even a Message translation and pursue knowing God. He just wants a relationship with us, and in our seeking, we will find Him.

She didn't know what to think but ended up sharing a lot more, so Dorothy and I ended up taking her hand and praying for her. It was absolutely beautiful. Then I felt like I was supposed to pray for a woman at the corner table and waited until she was done eating. Then I walked over and explained that I knew it was strange, but I was wondering if she needed healing or simply just a prayer. She looked at me with this shocked face (a lot of people do when I approach them), and she said that morning, the doctor found something wrong in her kidneys and wanted to do more tests. So I ended up praying for her, and to this day, I believe she was healed.

Soon after Dorothy and I finished our dinner, the young man who was the host and had his feet healed came over to our table. He said, "I know you said it's Jesus and all, but I don't understand." So I began to share the Gospel with him and asked him if he had ever physically felt the presence of God, and he replied by saying no. So I asked him if he would like to, and he said yes. What did I do? Well, I asked him if I could pray again, and he agreed. I placed my hand on his shoulder and asked Holy Spirit to come and make His presence known. I prayed that the Lord would touch His son so that His son would know that He was after a relationship with him and that it's not about me.

When I opened my eyes, tears were streaming down this young man's face, and the Lord had wrapped around him like a warm blanket. It's just amazing what the Lord will do to reach His lost sheep. What amazes me more is that He is so real and after us that most of the time, we just need a little "want to." The *want to* know Him. The *want to* experience Him. The desire to draw near to Him. He's there with open arms, but it is always our decision whether we turn to Him or not. It will always be our decision.

> **Many dishonest tax collectors and other notorious sinners often gathered around to listen as Jesus taught the people. This raised concerns among the Jewish religious leaders and experts of the law. Indignant, they grumbled and complained, saying, "Look at how this man associates with all these notorious sinners and welcomes them all to come to him!" In response, Jesus gave them this**

illustration: There once was a shepherd with a hundred lambs, but one of his lambs wandered away and was lost. So the shepherd left the ninety-nine lambs out in the open field and searched in the wilderness for that one lost lamb. He didn't stop until he finally found it. With exuberant joy he raised it up, placed it on his shoulders, and carried it back with cheerful delight! Returning home, he called all his friends and neighbors together and said, "Let's have a party! Come and celebrate with me the return of my lost lamb. It wandered away, but I found it and brought it home." Jesus continued, "In the same way, there will be a glorious celebration in heaven over the rescue of one lost sinner who repents, comes back home, and returns to the foldmore so than for all the righteous people who never strayed away." (Luke 15:1–7 TPT)

Dorothy and I were in *awe* of Father's move on this young man. I asked him if he would like to give his life to Jesus Christ. In tears, he nodded his head and said, "Yes." So right there in Applebee's, the young man gave his life and asked Jesus Christ to be his Lord and Savior.

It was moments like these that were continually happening to me, and I couldn't express what was going on inside my heart. It was like an explosion of love and compassion like I had never felt before in my life. Dorothy was overwhelmed as well and just wanted to spend as much time with me as possible. She kept telling me that I was bringing the book of Acts to life and really living out what the Lord calls us to. Dorothy also decided that she wanted to sponsor my trip to Texas for the upcoming Power and Love event that I had booked. She blessed me with a rental car, gas money, and money to get a hotel room. I was so grateful for her blessing me, and it made me more excited to attend the event because there was no denying God had provided for me yet again.

Dorothy had been a believer for over fifty years and would always tell me that she was so thankful to be growing and learning. It was as if she had no regrets about anything; she was just thankful. To be honest, she taught me so much, but one thing that I learned quickly from her was that this is a lifetime relationship with the Lord.

We will never have full understanding until we stand before Him. There is always something to learn and an opportunity to get closer to Him as each day passes. A relationship with the Lord isn't to get what we want but to draw close to the one who provides all we need. It is so much bigger than just believing in Him so we don't go to hell or getting our prayers answered. He paid an extremely high price for our freedom. It is ironic because, throughout these years, the hardest people to share my testimony with are religious people or those who have been in church for years. Most of the time, they see my tattoos and think the worst of me. Rather than recognizing that Jesus came for the broken, some feel you have to clean up before coming to Him. That's the complete opposite of what Jesus even taught.

Truth be told, I found peace when I realized that religious people are actually the ones who rejected Jesus. I know that I can't clean myself up. That is why I need God. I am washed by the blood, not people's religious traditions or opinions.

I still had and have a lot to learn. I'm thankful that God was not something I was just trying or a Father who gets angry when I make mistakes. Being His is a lifetime commitment, not something we just try to help ourselves. I am beyond thankful that He doesn't treat us the way we sometimes treat one another. He is so much more loving than that, and His grace is sufficient. Honestly, His mercy is new every single day, so if we messed up today, we are blessed to be able to repent and turn back to Him at any moment at any second. When we realize that what we have done is not in line with His will for our lives, He is faithful to forgive. Sounds too easy, I know. Religion has really distorted what a relationship truly is.

It is of the Lord's mercies that we are not consumed, because his compassions fail not. They are new every morning: great is thy faithfulness. (Lamentations 3:22–24 KJV)

This was actually the first holiday I spent sober in so many years that I couldn't even remember how long. Saint Patrick's Day was so much fun. Dorothy and I ended up going to the Muncie Mall to get this scented spray that I absolutely loved. As we walked into the bookstore to get to the main walkway of the mall, I was so full of energy and life. We walked out the door that entered the main walkway, and walking right in our direction was a young lady with crutches and a huge cast on her foot. It went all the way up to her knee, and I just stopped and stared at her. As she got closer to me, I asked her what happened. She explained that she had jumped off the tailgate of a truck and broken her ankle and had surgery scheduled for that Friday. I then proceeded to share my heart with her and that I believed that Jesus wanted her well.

Of course, her young boyfriend did what I see a lot, and he just rolled his eyes as I was speaking. I asked her if it would be okay to pray for her, and she said yes. So I then asked what her pain level was, with ten being the worse and zero being none. If I recall correctly, she said it was a twelve. I smiled and just kneeled down and touched her cast. I said, "In the name of Jesus Christ, bones and muscles, be healed right now." I then stood up and took a couple of steps back. I asked her to test it and see where the pain level was now. It was so cool because she took a few steps and then started to smile super big. She began freaking out a bit and then ran into me and hugged me. She said the pain was completely gone. It was amazing to see her reaction.

Many people don't expect anything to happen, but scripture is clear and tells us:

And these signs shall follow them that believe; In my name shall they cast out devils; they shall speak with new tongues; They shall take up

serpents; and if they drink any deadly things, it shall not hurt them; they shall lay hands on the sick, and they shall recover. (Mark 16:17 KJV)

I realized it wasn't about the faith of the person I was praying for. God's Word clearly says that these signs and wonders follow those who believe, and I believe with all my heart. I'm not going to claim that every single person I pray for gets healed, but I see more healing than not when I do pray. I am not claiming to have a full understanding of why some are healed and some are not; all I know is that God is good, and my trust and faith are in Him.

I have prayed for those whom I didn't see anything happen, and then an hour later, I would get a message sharing that their knee popped and was healed. It is all these moments I hold dear because it is not about what God is doing through me but what He is doing to a person's heart. He always hears our prayers, and I do not believe that any prayer goes void. So whether I see healing or not, I know Father is moving in that moment. It isn't always visible; sometimes it is way bigger than I could possibly understand.

During that time in my life, I was seeing more healings than I had ever even imagined possible.

As Dorothy and I continued on our journey in the mall, we walked into the store that had the scent spray I was after. There in front of the stand was a woman smelling all the scents, and she turned around holding one of the bottles and said, "Oh, you have to smell this." So I did. It was ironic because it just happened to be the exact scent, Candy Caramel Corn, that we had went into the store to get. I told her it smelled so good, not mentioning that I had come for that exact bottle.

As I began talking with the woman, I found out she was a volunteer at her church for mission trips, but this year, she wasn't allowed to go because she had a lump in her hand, and her shoulder was messed up. As we talked, I ended up asking her if I could pray for her, and she happily put her hand out and said yes. I took her hand and began commanding the lump to leave and for her shoulder to be healed in the mighty name of Jesus Christ, and right in front of our eyes, the lump completely went down and disappeared. Impossible, you say? I was there and saw it with my own eyes.

After the woman was healed, she began getting so loud and rejoicing, praising the Lord, and I soon realized that the lady behind the counter witnessed the entire thing. Everyone was looking at her hand in disbelief, and then the woman's daughter walked over pushing a stroller. The woman ran to her explaining what had happened and said, "I would show you the lump, but it's gone." It was indescribable as I realized and heard the girl behind the counter sharing with her coworker what she just witnessed Jesus do. I did end up stopping the woman and explaining that I didn't want to come across as deceiving and that I came for the exact scent she had me smell, and she just laughed at me. She was so overwhelmed and filled with so much joy. It was a fun day, to say the least.

Dorothy and I would spend most of our day praising and talking about how good the Lord was. We spent almost every day together, and I was so thankful to have a sister in Christ who wasn't judging me or making fun of me. We would look up, talk about, and share scripture with each other consistently. She shared with me how she had watched ministries on TV for years, but she had never personally known someone who was actually walking it out.

When I would pray for someone, Dorothy would always lift her hand toward the person and begin to pray quietly with me. She was such a huge encourager, and she shared so many testimonies in her Bible study groups that at one point Sally told her she was concerned that it sounded like Dorothy was idolizing me. Dorothy, however, was quick to point out that even Paul said:

I want you to pattern your lives after me, just as I pattern mine after Christ. (1 Corinthians 11:1 TPT)

Dorothy explained that I was living my life following Jesus, and He received all the glory. She told Sally she wasn't idolizing me; she was sharing about what Christ in me was doing through me. I think in a strange way that Sally was a little jealous of the growing friendship Dorothy and I were blessed with. Sally began saying even stranger things to me like she *used* to heal others "for a season" and other things that I didn't see in scripture. I didn't understand because I did look up to Sally, but I knew that some of the things she said were not in line with the Word. I just knew one thing for sure, and that was I was called to love her, not judge her.

I confess that some of the things she would say would leave me questioning the scripture, but I had to grow in realizing that people are not who I am to follow. Jesus is the way, the truth, and the life. It is crazy how our opinions and others will tend to be placed higher than the truth. It doesn't change the truth, but it does try to distort it when we place more value on the opinions of others above what God says.

I never realized how much others used scripture to hurt others. It truly saddens my heart when others try to take on the role of God while claiming and justifying their judgment in the name of Jesus.

It took some really hot fires, trials, and lessons for me to grow into understanding that I am not what others may think. I'm also not in charge of anyone else's salvation, and when I stand before the Lord, as we all will, He is not going to ask me why you did something. I will have to answer for my heart—for the words that came out of my mouth.

We are all called to share the Gospel as followers of Jesus Christ. However, our gifting, our opinions, and our experiences are not the Gospel. Those things can encourage others in faith, but they are not our identity, and they definitely don't replace the good news of Jesus Christ.

Do not scoff at prophecies, but test everything that is said. Hold on to what is good. (1 Thessalonians 5:20–21 NLT)

CHAPTER 6

THE FREEDOM

April 2018

On April 1, I began my journey down to Texas. I planned on spending eight days in the woods camping and then going to my hotel for the four-day conference. My plan was to fast and spend eight days straight with no electricity and no food—just me and the Lord. With my Bible packed and my tent ready to go, I headed out on the road. I was about two and a half hours into my trip when I received a call from Bree. She was staying with her best friend, and their dog had attacked her and bit her face. Bree began telling me that when she went to the bathroom and cleaned the wound, she had placed a towel over her cheek where the dog had bit her. When she went to look in the mirror, she said a huge piece of her cheek was hanging. I instantly told Bree to keep her hand there, and we began to pray.

Once we finished praying, I asked Bree if she wanted me to turn around, and she said, "No, Mom. I will be okay. I know you're supposed to go on this trip, and I don't want anything to stop you." I kept asking if she was sure, and she just kept telling me she would be okay. She was heading to the hospital and told me she would keep me posted.

As I continued driving, I just began speaking over my daughter and praying for the Lord's favor to overwhelm and surround her. It wasn't long before Bree called me back and let me know she only needed a few stitches. She was so overjoyed because she swore her cheek was way worse before we had prayed. We both thanked the Lord and began to just praise Him for His goodness and mercy.

I arrived in Texas at my campsite on Monday, April 2, and couldn't have been more excited. I was ready to get my tent set up and sit back to read my Bible. I had been blessed with a cabin tent, and it was huge. The instructions stated that it recommended two people to set up, but there I was, all alone. I got the tent set up by the grace of God, and then it was time to put the roof cover on. I tried everything I could to get it on top of the tent to no avail. It was so wild because I had no idea how I was going to be able to make it work. Then the thought came to me that reminded me of James 4:2, "You receive not because you ask not." So I simply said to the Lord, "I know this is silly, but I need help right now. I can't put this top on by myself, Lord. Please send someone I can ask to help me." As soon as I finished saying that, with the cover in my hand, the wind began to pick up. I literally said, "No WAY." I began allowing the wind to lift the cover, and it was enough to actually get the thing over the top of my tent and latch it down in the corners.

Things that seem impossible like this were happening to me so much that I didn't even share certain things with others because I thought they would think I was crazy. Even as I type all of this now, I have thoughts about how I shouldn't share because of the opinions some will have of me. Yet I also know what happened, so it isn't about convincing others what happened. I'm not trying to argue with anyone over what or why I experienced the things I did. I may not be believed, but I can't be unconvinced because I was there and know the truth. My heart is truly to bring God glory, and my prayer is that my testimony encourages others to know that all things are possible when we surrender to Jesus Christ.

And he who has seen has testified, and his testimony is true; and he knows that he is telling the truth, so that you may believe. (John 19:35 NKJV)

To God be all the glory.
Once my campsite was set up, I settled in with my Bible and relaxed. It was so beautiful where I was, and my tent was near a huge lake, so the view was awesome. During my first few days, I simply fasted and spent time with the Lord. I love reading His Word and just spending time in study. Finally, one day, the Lord told me to break my fast. I remember saying out loud, "Are you sure?" as if God doesn't know what He is doing.

So I went ahead and headed to a restaurant near me. I was sitting alone when all of a sudden, a woman walked past me and just turned around to stare right at me. I simply smiled and asked her if she was there alone, and she said that she was. I knew instantly it was a divine meeting, and I invited her to join me. She was from Oklahoma and had rented a cabin in the area so she could attend a Shawn Bolz conference. We talked for a couple of hours and really just shared Jesus and scripture with each other. It was incredible after I got back to my tent because I realized I would have never met her if I was not listening and stayed in my tent as I had planned.

That night, I had the most vivid, detailed dream that rocked me. I am not one to usually have dreams, and I am definitely not one to write my dreams down. I do believe that the Lord will speak to us through our dreams. However, I tend to feel that if He is trying to tell me something in a dream, I will remember it. I know of several people who will wake up to write down what they've dreamed. I can honestly say that I am not that person. I think I have had maybe three really prophetic dreams that I knew were of the Lord. One of which, I even had an amazing artist paint for me.

Anyway, on this night, I dreamed that I was with a very dear friend, and we were talking about the Lord, and I was sharing my testimony with her. All of a sudden, she asked me to pray for her, and, of course, I did. As soon as I started praying, she began manifesting a demon, growling and falling to the floor. It was so intense. I can remember it like it was yesterday. In my dream, that demon left, and there was freedom.

I woke up jumping up and down. It almost felt like my heart was going to beat out of my chest, and all I could say was, "Yes, Lord. Yes!" I called Dorothy to share with her what happened, and it was almost like she was more excited than I was.

I loved sharing with Dorothy. I made a few videos to share on my social media while I was at my campsite. Then one day while I was reading, my phone rang, and it was a friend who I hadn't spoken to in over twenty-five years. I lived near him when I was younger and lived in Las Cruces, New Mexico. He was a young man who I had boxed and knocked out when I was in Butterfield Park, referenced in *Broken Not Shattered*. It was such a surprise, but he told me that he had been watching my videos and could always feel the presence of the Lord when he did. It was such an encouraging phone call. He asked if he could put his friend, Jezzy, in touch with me because they were running a work release program for some women who were incarcerated, and he felt my book would be perfect for their group.

By day eight, I was so fired up I could barely contain myself. I had so many revelations while I was in the woods with the Lord. It was an unforgettable time. To this day, I love going to the woods and camping. There is something about being outdoors that makes me feel closer to the Lord. I was so thankful for my time and really felt like it had gone fast. After packing up my campsite, I jumped in the car and was off to the hotel. Once I arrived, I settled in and decided I wanted to get a good seat at the Power and Love, so my plan was to show up super early and just wait by the door. Eventually, I set my alarm and went to sleep.

When I arrived at Lifestyle Christianity University in Watauga, Texas, I couldn't express the way my heart was pounding. I didn't know what to expect, but I knew that the Lord had led me there, so it had to be good. On the first day, I ended up meeting so many people and just loved getting to hang out with others who were on fire for the Lord. There was some of the best worship music I had ever heard live, and then it happened. A woman sat next to me, and she was so different that at one point, I literally asked Father, "Really, Lord?" Talk about me being a little bit judgmental. I was seeing people get "slain in the spirit," having "holy laughter," and many things I had no idea what to think. I had never seen anything like this. The woman next to me would shake and almost act like she was having an orgasm, which was so weird to me. I just thought, *You know what, Lord, you're not in a box, and I'm not here to judge.*

By the end of the evening, the woman next to me, Esther, ended up asking me if I would save a seat for her the next day. She offered to buy me lunch for doing it because she knew that I planned to be there around 6:00 a.m. even though the doors didn't open until like 8:30 a.m. I really didn't want to do it because she almost annoyed me, but I told her I would save her a seat and that there was no need to buy me lunch. I went to my hotel that night and dove straight into my Bible. There were so many good things said throughout the night that I didn't want to miss anything. I wrote a ton of notes and began praying just asking Father for understanding and wisdom in what I was seeing and hearing. Some of the notes I took were as follows:

> **Don't allow sin against you to produce sin in you.**
>
> **Your calling is to suffer for doing good and not let it change you.**
>
> **Godly contentment comes from knowing who you are, not from stuff of this world.**
>
> **Jesus became unrecognizable so that we may be recognizable. We need to see the price He paid.**
>
> **There is no grace outside of Jesus.**
>
> **You have to give up your right to understanding.**
>
> **When you are under attack, counteract with praying for others.**
>
> **(These quotes are from different speakers at the event!)**

There were so many good things stated, and they all pointed to Jesus. I had never heard some of the things that were said, but there was a lot of scripture spoken. At the event, set up outside was a protester who had literally made a huge sign with flames that said, "Todd White and Heidi Baker are going to hell." It was announced, and we were asked not to approach the protester because he recorded it all and would post videos twisting a lot of what anyone said. I know that while I was standing outside, the guy was speaking on his megaphone and said so many mean things and judgmental things that my chest was lit with fire, not in anger at all. Each time he would say something, there was like a physical fire on me, and I didn't understand it. All I know is that the presence of the Lord tends to touch me like that sometimes.

I saw so many things I didn't understand, but I wasn't bothered by my not understanding. I just wanted to know the Lord more. I just let go of some of the things said in one ear and out the other because I either didn't understand or just didn't fully agree. They wanted to send everyone out to pray for others, but since I had been living that way already, I just ended up enjoying time with other conference goers.

Esther did end up buying me lunch, and to my surprise, we ended up becoming friends. She wasn't as annoying as I had felt, plus I really prayed about it because I felt bad for being annoyed. It's so funny how some would say, "That's not very Christian of you, Zara, being annoyed by someone." Please, if you really believe Jesus never got annoyed, you should consider reading the Bible.

> **Then Jesus answered and said, "O faithless and perverse generation, how long shall I be with you? How long shall I bear with you? Bring him here to Me." (Matthew 17:17 NKJV)**

Or when He spoke to Peter and said:

> **Jesus turned to Peter and said, "Get out of my way, you Satan! You are a hindrance to me,**

because your thoughts are only filled with man's viewpoints and not with the ways of God." (Matthew 16:23 TPT)

There are many other examples of Jesus rebuking others, but it wasn't like it was from a place of hatred. Jesus loved, Jesus was love, and Jesus is love. It's not like worldly love, "butterflies," blah, blah. Just like butterflies, that worldly love eventually flies away.

One of the many things that stayed with me from this conference was when Heidi Baker said, "Love looks like something." Love is an action! Just read 1 Corinthians 13 if you need a better understanding. Love never stops loving. It isn't selfish like we usually walk in, saying, "I love you," just to hear, "I love you," back. Nope, it is much deeper and more real than that.

At one point, while waiting for the conference to start back up after one of our breaks, there was a guy behind me who was talking to his friend. He was telling his friend that he was still not sure about all this and that he had several people pray for him, but nothing happened. I, of course, was curious and turned around and started talking to him. His name was Dennis, and he was a father of seven from Canada. He was there because he was curious about having a relationship with Jesus and wanted to understand more. He was hungry for truth just like I was.

I asked him what was wrong with him, and he told me about his knee and back being messed up. So with a heart to see him healed, I did the only thing I knew and asked him if I could pray for him. He was open to it. I just laid my hand on him and prayed for the Lord to touch him. I then began to command his knee and back to be healed in Jesus mighty name. I asked him to see if anything was changed, and he started checking. All of a sudden, his eyes got bigger, and he said he had to go to the bathroom to really check.

I was anticipating his return because, by this time, I had seen so many people touched by the Lord. I just had no doubt that God did something. When he returned, he was so excited and almost in tears. It was finished; he was healed. He even reached forward at one point with his phone to show me that he had texted his wife that Jesus healed his knee and back. It was so much fun to be there and be a part of that.

Dennis and I are still in touch, and I have had the blessing of meeting his beautiful wife and some of their children. I believe they have nine now. They are raising an army of giant killers. The connections I made at that conference were so amazing. and I still speak to many of the people I met there.

As the days went on, I couldn't explain the things I learned, and the things I saw were even more incredible. As I listened to Todd White, I agreed with a lot of what he was teaching. He didn't seem to yell as I had seen in videos; he was intense, but it was a beautiful intensity for the Lord. It was funny because at one point, Heidi Baker asked people who wanted prayer to come forward, and I definitely headed up. I was standing there, and this woman, who was on Heidi's team, was walking down the line praying for people, and they would fall back to the floor. She came to me and placed her hand on my head and began pushing me down. I reached up because I was going to grab her arm and push her away, but something stopped me. I guess I felt like it would be rude or something. I appeased her and fell backward, but I instantly sat up completely confused about why she would push me like that. I thought perhaps that is why people were falling down. I learned in time, though, that sometimes, it is the power of Holy Spirit because I refuse to push people and have had it happen many times when I've prayed over people.

I guess another woman saw what happened because she came next to me and started telling me that God loved me. The entire experience confused me because I had never been a part of anything like that, and I couldn't understand the point of forcing people to fall down. That didn't seem like Holy Spirit or anything Father would do.

Honestly, some of the things I saw didn't make any sense to me because I read that self-control is part of the fruit of the Spirit. Yet some of the things I was seeing had zero self-control involved. To this day, I have no doubt that the Lord can do anything. I've learned not to judge people if they have a different reaction to Holy Spirit, but I have witnessed some amazing things and some demonic things. It is so important that we learn to use discernment in all things.

> **Beloved, do not believe every spirit, but test the spirits, whether they are of God; because many false prophets have gone out into the world. By this you know the Spirit of God: Every spirit that confesses that Jesus Christ has come in the flesh is of God, and every spirit that does not confess that Jesus Christ has come in the flesh is not of God. And this is the spirit of the Antichrist, which you have heard was coming and is now already in the world. You are of God, little children, and have overcome them, because He who is in you is greater than he who is in the world. (1 John 4:1–4 NKJV)**

At another time, we were all worshipping at the conference, and a song that I had never heard before began playing. It was called "Surrounded." I absolutely loved it. Ironically, it only has a few verses that repeat in the song, and that is pretty much all there is to it; but for some reason, this song just stayed with me all night. It did something to my heart the very first time I heard it. Two verses to the song are, "This is how I fight my battles," and, "It may look like I'm surrounded, but I'm surrounded by you."

When I got back to the hotel later that night, I got on YouTube and looked up the song. I somehow connected that the song was in reference to the Bible verse as follows:

> **The Spirit of the Sovereign Lord is on me, because the Lord has anointed me to proclaim good news to the poor. He has sent me to bind up the brokenhearted, to proclaim freedom**

> **for the captives and release from darkness for the prisoners, to bestow on them a crown of beauty instead of ashes, the oil of joy instead of mourning, and a garment of praise instead of a spirit of despair. They will be called oaks of righteousness, a planting of the Lord for the display of his splendor. (Isaiah 61:1–3 NIV)**

Praise God. At that moment, I could see so clearly that all of my past, all of the ashes of my life, were becoming beauty. I was truly being made new. I realized what being set free truly meant, and it wasn't me controlling anything. It was actually me completely surrendering everything to Jesus Christ. I just had the song put on repeat and meditated deeply on the words I was reading in scripture over and over. I knew that it was praising our Lord and Savior in the midst of the storms. That was key and exactly how we overcome our battles. I fell asleep listening to this song and knew that Isaiah 61:3 was a verse that was meant for me at that exact moment in my life. He really turned my ashes into beauty.

When I woke up the next morning, a sister in Christ, whom I had only spoken to a couple of times on the phone, had texted me the exact same verse, Isaiah 61:3; and it was completely typed out. I almost dropped my phone. She had no idea about what happened the night before or how relevant that verse was to me, and yet, there she was, texting the exact scripture to me. Out of all the verses in the Bible, what were the chances she would take the time to text me the exact verse I was meditating on all night? I'm telling you. It was like I was in an entirely different world. I knew God really cared for me in a way I had never imagined. I saw proof all around me when before it was almost as if my eyes were closed as I went through life. I suppose you could say they were closed.

Now throughout the entire conference, I had at least a dozen people come up to me and ask me if I had been to Upper Room. I had no idea what they were talking about, and after simply saying, "No," a bunch of times, I finally asked, "What is it?" I was told it was a church located in Dallas. I kept being told that I needed to go before heading back to Indiana, so I took that as a sign.

It amazes me how we will ignore so many signs that God is speaking to us because it comes through other people. I did the same until I realized and understood that God does use others to bless, speak, and show up in our lives in huge ways.

So the plan was in motion. I was going to attend church at Upper Room in Dallas, Sunday morning before heading back on the road. There were so many other things that happened at this conference that if I were to try to share it all, it would take up most of this book. Let me just close this with the fact that when I left the Power and Love, prayers were answered, I had a better understanding, and the biggest thing I took away from it was the fact that I wasn't alone. Others were just as on fire as I was, and they were made fun of by those they loved too. I talked to others who had families reject them because they gave their life to Christ and some who were made fun of daily. It made me realize that we truly are in the world, but we are not of it. In the presence of the Lord, we are always home. That's why He says to keep our minds on things above.

> **Since, then, you have been raised with Christ, set your hearts on things above, where Christ is, seated at the right hand of God. Set your minds on things above, not on earthly things. (Colossians 3:1–2 NIV)**

On Sunday morning, I was packed and ready to head to church. It had already been an incredibly unforgettable trip, but I knew there was more in store for me. The church wasn't too far from my hotel. I think it was about a forty-five-minute drive, so I made sure to leave early. It was a good thing that I did because traffic in the Dallas–Fort Worth (DFW) area is absolutely insane.

I am not much of a city girl, so it was not fun driving in all that madness. I got to the church and was sitting about four rows back from the front. I listened intently, and the message was really good. There was a lot of reassurance for me on things that I was already seeing in scripture. Then it happened. I was blown completely away. The pastor said, with an authoritative voice, "I want you to take your ashes and lay them at the feet of Jesus. He is turning your ashes into beauty!" I almost lost my balance and fell out of my chair. Did he really just say that? I'm not sure I heard anything else he said after that because my heart was pounding, and my mind was trying to wrap around how much God was doing in my life. God was speaking directly to me, and there was no denying it.

A few minutes later, we were dismissed, and I began putting my coat on. This beautiful young lady approached me and asked me what my name was. As I grabbed her hand to shake it, I told her my name was Zara. All of a sudden, she began to tell me that the Lord had highlighted me to her throughout the entire sermon. She said, "The Lord wants you to know that He sees you. What you are thinking He is going to use you for is not even close. He is going to use you astronomically bigger than you're thinking. You are going to be His solider on the front lines. He is preparing your heart and loves you."

I just stared at her as the tears began to swell in my eyes. I thanked her for being obedient and coming to me. What else do you say at that point?

As soon as I made it to the car, I lost it. I just sat there sobbing as I thanked God for loving me and for truly seeing me. I then wrote everything she said down so I didn't forget.

After I pulled myself together, I started the car and headed back into the crazy traffic. I was blown away and just kept saying out loud, "Is this real? Is this all really happening?" Then out of nowhere, a semitruck pulled in front of me on the highway. I literally had to slam on my brakes and completely slow down. When I was done freaking out, I looked up. Now I was a carnie (traveled with the carnival for years) and have traveled all of my life. I mean, at a young age, I would literally do the arm gesture to get semitrucks to honk their horns. I've seen more highways than most folks other than truck drivers, of course. I had never seen a truck with scripture on it until that day.

I looked up, and there it was. On the back of this semitruck that pulled in front of me were the words, in big letters, "Trust," with the words, "Isaiah 40:31." I was so taken back that I grabbed my phone and took a quick picture. I drove far enough to get out of the city, but I stopped early that day because I was so ready to read what that verse was, and I really needed to just rest. I was so overwhelmed by the entire trip and all that had been happening over the past couple of months. Here is what the scripture says:

But they that wait upon the Lord shall renew their strength; they shall mount up with wings as eagles; they shall run, and not be weary; and they shall walk, and not faint. (Isaiah 40:31 KJV)

I made a video in my hotel room that night because when I checked into my room, I had a great experience with the lady working there. When I walked into the hotel, I instantly felt Father's love for the woman behind the counter. I felt like the Lord wanted me to pray for her knee, so I began asking her about her knee. She was so confused but confessed that she had been having trouble in her knee and was scheduled for an MRI. I then asked her if I could pray for her, and she agreed. So I took her hand and began praying.

When I was finished, I asked her to check her knee; and to her surprise, she said that it wasn't making the sound or popping the way that it had been. I asked her how the pain was, and she shared that it didn't even hurt as much. I then went ahead and asked if I could pray again, and she agreed.

As I was praying, I felt a nudge to pray for her back as well. I didn't even ask. I just began praying for her back pain as well. As soon as I was finished, the woman was almost in tears as she asked me how I could possibly know about her back issue. I explained that I love the Lord and that He is always speaking if we would just listen. I simply shared that the Lord adored her and that He truly wanted a relationship with her. After that, I was so wired up I could barely sleep. I read my Bible and continued to reflect on everything I was experiencing and witnessing.

There is no power above or beneath us—no power that could ever be found in the universe that can distance us from God's passionate love, which is lavished upon us through our Lord Jesus, the Anointed One! (Romans 8:39 TPT)

I arrived back at my trailer on Monday, and I was so glad to be back in Indiana. I didn't even unpack. I just went straight to Dorothy's house and began sharing all that had happened on my trip. She was excited with me, and everything seemed so unreal. After I shared for hours with Dorothy, I gave her a hug and headed home.

The next morning, when I woke up, I received a strange phone call. The number was not programmed in my phone, and it said it was from Texas. When I answered it, the voice on the other end said, "Zara, in prayer this morning, the Lord told me that because the devil can't get to you, he is going to try to attack your family. I am just calling to warn you so you can be prepared." I was so taken back that all I could say was, "Thank you," and the call ended.

To this day, I still have no idea who it was that called me, but about an hour and a half later after the call, my mother called. She told me she had been thinking about suicide and even drinking, which was a surprise since my mother wasn't a drinker. I told her that I would come straight to Michigan and explained that I hadn't even unpacked from my trip, so it was not a problem. She was extremely hesitant and said she didn't want to be a bother, but I told her that all I knew was that Jesus was amazing, and I would come pray for her and the house. I told her I wouldn't come up unless she said she wanted me to; eventually, she agreed and asked me to come.

When I arrived at my mother's, we ended up going to dinner. I just shared with her all the amazing things I was witnessing and the things I was growing in. I shared that God is good and wants us well. I'm not sure she believed me, but she was listening to the best of her ability. She shared with me that she had been watching Kingdom Living with Dan Mohler on YouTube.

Her notebook was full of notes, and she said that she was fighting because the devil was convincing her that I was lying about all that I had been sharing with her. She even showed me her notebook where the things she had written down had lines through them with the word *devil* above them. It was crazy to me. I just loved her and wasn't sure how to respond to the things she was saying. Somewhere along the way, she was extremely twisted and felt my life was something to compete with. It was and still is heartbreaking. I'm not hurt by her anymore. I honestly hurt for her.

When we got back from dinner, she was sitting on the couch, and I asked her if I could pray for her. She shared that she was having supernatural experiences in the house. See, my grandmother passed away in that house in April 2017. I believe that her demons were now wandering around that house tormenting my mother. No, I can't explain it or have proof. All I knew was what I felt like the Lord was revealing to me. My mother described how her bed would get a physical impression on it as if someone had sat down and how she would talk to it like it was her mom or her deceased husband. I knew from reading scripture that it was a big no, no. The Bible is actually pretty clear on certain things that we like to do to make ourselves comfortable, and speaking to the dead is one of them.

Refer to the following: **1 Samuel 28:6–11; 1 Chronicles 10:9–14; Leviticus 19:31; Galatians 5:19–21; Micah 5:12; Deuteronomy 18:10–14; and Ecclesiastes 9:4–6 just to name a few.**

I didn't know much and still don't, but what I do know is that the scripture does not say that the dead come to visit us nor are we to have conversations with them and ask things of them. Jesus is the only way, the only truth, and the only life. Scripture even says:

> **Life, lovely while it lasts, is soon over. Life as we know it, precious and beautiful, ends. The body is put back in the same ground it came from. The spirit returns to God who first breathed it. (Ecclesiastes 12:6–7 MSG)**

I believe that what we consider "ghosts" of our past loved ones can actually be demons. I believe they are tricksters and come in different forms. We have this crazy idea that the devil is red with horns or super scary looking because we have been conditioned that way through movies and the like. I do not believe this to be true, but that is something I encourage you to pray on and take to Father.

After explaining my heart on all of this to my mother, I felt the only thing to do was pray and invite God to do what only He could. When I laid my hand on my mom, she began to feel an intense warmth all over her body. She smiled and said she felt Holy Spirit. I led her in prayer, and she asked the Lord to come into her heart and to be her Lord and Savior. Soon after, she asked me if I could pray over the house.

I confess, I had been speaking to her for hours about her authority and how she needed to rise up, so I told her, "Yes, Mom, but you can pray for the house yourself. All you have to do is—" and I closed my eyes and began commanding any unclean spirits to leave. I proclaimed the blood of Jesus over the house, and when I opened my eyes, I was almost knocked back, literally.

There was like this supernatural bang. The instant my eyes opened, it was like an explosion. This is so hard to put into words. There was a complete holy utterance and shift in the house. My jaw dropped, and I looked at my mom with my eyes as wide open as they possibly could have been. I said, "Did you feel that?"

She nodded her head yes, and it was done. After that experience, my mom never had another "visitor" in that house again. She told me later that the voices had stopped, and she didn't have suicidal thoughts again either. I can't say where she is now, but I will explain more of that later on.

On April 19, 2018, I arrived home from my trip to Michigan. Ironically, I was meeting with several women a week to just minister and answer any questions they had. I can't explain how or why God placed me in that position, but others were seeing how much my life had changed. A woman approached me unexpectedly and said, "Zara, I know this may sound crazy, but the Holy Spirit told me in prayer last night that I am to pay all of your debt in full. I need you to get any bills you have together, and I would like to pay them. Any and all bills, whether in collection, student loans, whatever you owe."

Yeah, you think you're in unbelief? I didn't know what was happening or if it was even real. I believe I even looked behind myself to make sure the woman wasn't speaking to someone else. I began crying and was lost for words.

It took me a couple of days to even believe it. I had all kinds of crazy thoughts. I was raised that you work for what you have, so you owe no one anything. This couldn't be really happening; there had to be an angle, right? I was honestly allowing my pride to get in the way of a blessing sent to me from the Lord. It was when I was sitting on my couch reflecting on what the woman had said that the Lord spoke as clearly as could be to me. He said, "What are you doing? I've sent someone to help you."

In that instant, I just replied to Him and said, "Okay." I started getting every bill and every single debt I had together—student loans, past bills, credit cards, everything. It all came out to about $55,000. When I saw the total amount, I thought, *For sure, this wasn't going to happen.* Who in their right mind is just going to give me $55,000 to help me with no expectations of something in return. Yet on April 23, 2018, every dime I owed to anyone or any company was mailed out and paid in full with no contingencies.

It wasn't long after when someone came up to me and said, "Zara, I am supposed to buy you a truck, and would like you to find the one you want? I want to bless you." What was happening? I didn't even understand what to do other than say thank you and cry. Soon, I was driving off a car lot with a 2018 Chevy Silverado, 2500HD, High-Country Duramax, and it was in my name as the legal owner. The truck was almost $65,000 and was paid for with nothing expected from me. I literally named the truck "The Kings Chariot" because I knew that where the Lord called me, I would go. Then I was blessed with a brand-new travel trailer paid in full and a brand-new HP laptop that was worth $1,800, with the encouraging words that I was going to write another book.

At the end of April, I was debt-free, had a new truck and new trailer, a new laptop, and a little money in the bank. I know I keep saying it, but I seriously can't explain why or how the things that happened in my life happened the way they did. I am not someone super special or have something others don't. I am a believer in Jesus Christ, and Holy Spirit lives inside of me.

If you're a believer, you have all that I have. My life got even wilder. Hold on to your seat (or the book). I am going to simply end this chapter by saying God can do what you think is impossible. My life is the transparent truth and testimony of that!

CHAPTER 7

THE MIRACLE

May 2018

Needless to say, my entire life was changed, and my family saw every bit of it. My daughter was truly seeing the difference in me and my life lived. There was no denying the Lord was changing me and blessing me in huge ways. One day, Bree saw Robby Dawkins on YouTube as I was watching him and said she really would like to meet that man. So I looked online and found out he was going to be a guest speaker at a different Power and Love conference in June that was to be held in Michigan. Dorothy and my mother also wanted to go with us, so I booked the tickets and a couple of hotel rooms for Grand Rapids, Michigan.

One day, as Bree was out with her best friend, I received a video message. It was Bree, kneeling down next to a man on a curb. Her best friend sent me the video and explained that they were driving, and a guy was on his moped, and a car just hit him right in front of them. My daughter, my sweet precious daughter, went over to him after the girls pulled over, and she ended up praying for the man. Her friend took a video of the entire thing from their car that was parked across the street. I can't express how filled my heart was at that exact moment. Bree was seeing how good God is, and she was believing.

> **And if anyone longs to be wise, ask God for wisdom and he will give it! He won't see your lack of wisdom as an opportunity to scold you over your failures but he will overwhelm your failures with his generous grace. Just make sure you ask empowered by confident faith without doubting that you will receive. For the ambivalent person believes one minute and doubts the next. Being undecided makes you become like the rough seas driven and tossed by the wind. You're up on minute and tossed down the next. When you are half-hearted and wavering, it leaves you unstable. Can you really expect to receive anything from the Lord when you're in that condition. (James 1:5–8 TPT)**

It was around this time that I was introduced to the Wanderlust movie *Furious Love* by Darren Wilson. I'll never forget putting the movie into my DVD player and how my chest literally filled with the tangible fire of Holy Spirit within the very first fifteen minutes of the movie. I ended up dropping to my knees and praying to the Lord something like, "I am yours, Lord. My life is yours. Use me as you want!" The movie rocked me to my core.

I want to take a moment here to say that I realize all of this can be stretching to the mind. It can seem impossible or downright ridiculous. Trust me, I understand. If all of this hadn't happened to me personally, I would feel the same way. However, it did happen to me, and I can't deny the freedom in just surrendering everything—all of my dreams and my life—to the Lord. We are here for Him, and all He asks in return is everything.

There is this false gospel that makes it sound like things will get so easy and life will just be peachy cream when we ask Jesus Christ to be our Savior. I assure you; He wants all of us, every part, even the dirty stuff, broken things, everything. So what does it cost you to follow Jesus? Just everything you weren't created for to begin with because you weren't created to live for yourself. You have a purpose, and it is to bring God glory—to be the hands and feet of Jesus here on earth as it is in heaven. I have zero interest in debating opinions or theology. I just believe in my Bible and love my relationship with the Lord. He doesn't fit in any of our boxes or our opinions:

> **I don't think the way you think. The way you work isn't the way I work. God's Decree. For as the sky soars high above earth, so the way I work surpasses the way you work, and the way I think is beyond the way you think. Just as rain and snow descend from the skies and don't go back until they've watered the earth, doing their work of making things grow and blossom, producing seed for farmers and food for the hungry, So will the words that come out of my mouth not come back empty-handed. They'll do the work I sent them to do, they'll complete the assignment I gave them. (Isaiah 55:8–11 MSG)**

> **Do not deceive yourselves. If any of you think you are wise by the standards of this age, you should become "fools" so that you may become wise. For the wisdom of this world is foolishness in God's sight. As it is written: "He catches the wise in their craftiness"; and again, "The Lord knows that the thoughts of the wise are futile." (1 Corinthians 3:18–20 NIV)**

I began to start hearing rumors about my little brother making fun of me. I wasn't allowed around my niece as much because my brother's girlfriend didn't want me to talk about Jesus. She didn't even like being around me either because I couldn't really talk about anything else. I didn't even watch TV anymore.

I started to see and feel so much rejection around me. A lot of people were supporting my changes and what God was doing, but there were so many others who had jealousy because of my blessings. I didn't boast about the financial things and even stopped making so many videos because I was concerned about the hatred and jealousy of others. That is one thing I believe I would change now if I could, but I guess I am because here I am, writing a book confessing it all. There are always going to be haters, but what I have learned is that our war is not flesh and blood. Therefore, when someone rejects me, I just look at it as if they are rejecting the kingdom within me. I don't see people as my enemy anymore; the devil and his demons are the only enemies I have, and their ending has already been written. The victory has already been won.

> **Be well balanced and always alert, because your enemy, the devil, roams around incessantly, like a roaring lion looking for its prey to devour. Take a decisive stand against him and resist his every attack with strong, vigorous faith. For you know that your believing brothers and sisters around the world are experiencing the same kinds of troubles you endure. (1 Peter 5:8–9 TPT)**

I spent a lot of time alone in tears, just praising and thanking God. I can't tell you how many times or how long I would just sit in awe, crying and just praising the Lord for what He did for me on that cross and for what He was doing in my life. There were many moments I laid flat on my face asking the Lord to never allow money to change me. I want and wanted to honor Him with my life lived, and I was willing to do anything He wanted me to. I heard a speaker one time share this story about a "chicken lady." That is the faith I want to walk in. The speaker said:

There was a preacher giving a sermon, and all of a sudden, right in the middle of the sermon, a woman stood up and started clucking like a chicken. Everyone looked at her, some with disgust, others with just shock, then she sat back down in her seat. Startled, and not sure what to do with it, the preacher just continued with his sermon. At the end the preacher did an altar call and asked if anyone wanted to give their life to Christ. After a few minutes the congregation heard over the loud speaker, "Hold on, please listen to this church." There was a man that took the microphone and said that he told the Lord he was done. That he had a plan to take his life that night, but he made a deal with God; that if he made someone stand up and cluck like a chicken, he would live the rest of his life for the Lord. (Author unknown)

When I heard that story, I literally began and still pray on occasion, "Lord, let me live my life like the chicken lady." Can you imagine? If the Lord told you to stand up in the middle of a sermon and cluck like a chicken, would you? The world would think it was crazy or rude, but God doesn't follow our rules. It reminds me of the faith of Noah, building an ark while everyone around him judged him and made fun of him. I just want to live my life with that kind of faith—not questioning everything the Lord says just because it might be out of my comfort zone but walking in faith that He knows what is best and has a plan! My heart's desire is to let my life reflect His love. That doesn't mean perfection as some religious folks think. It definitely is bigger than me. A mistake I had to grow from was learning that my identity is not found in my gifting or my calling. My identity is only found in Jesus.

For the gifts and calling of God are without repentance. (Romans 11:29 KJV)

I had a friend reach out to me who I hadn't spoken with except for a couple of hours the previous year in over seventeen years. Her name is Ruth. She said she was struggling with her faith. She called it a "faith crisis." Ruth told me she had been following me online and felt the Lord wanted her to reach out to me. I instantly felt like we were supposed to get together and invited her to come spend a weekend with me. She agreed and said she had to set up a sitter for her animals and would call me when she was able to come down. Eventually, we set the date for her visit for May 27–29.

I was experiencing many things for the first time, and being sober during holidays was one of them. It was strange for me, and I didn't know what to do when it came to the holidays. The week before Memorial Day, Dorothy was sharing with me how she wanted to put flowers on her parents' and aunts', and uncles' graves. It was different for me as I have never done that before, but it is really a thing. So I offered to help her, and she spent over $200 on fake flowers, which simply blew me away. Mind you, I lived in poverty most of my life, and that was a lot of money to me. We headed out to the graveyard, and I began to do as she asked, putting flowers where she said and using wire to attach them.

I know it sounds weird, but we had so much fun. I kept teasing her and asking, "Is this really what *normal* people do for Memorial Day? I used to barbecue and drink, and you think I was crazy while *normal people* are over here putting flowers on graves where your loved ones aren't even at."

She just kept laughing at me when I would say, "This is so strange. Normal people are so weird." I was, of course, just having fun and making her laugh a lot. I loved Dorothy's laugh; she was such an amazing woman of God. Although Dorothy was in her seventies, I never saw her age. She was so young at heart and truly became my best friend. She was a sister I had always wanted, and I could never express in words how very much I loved her. We had so many adventures together that I couldn't even write them all down.

The day quickly came when I was supposed to pick up Ruth and bring her down to my trailer for the weekend. On the morning of May 27, 2018, I woke up and instantly knew that Bree was supposed to leave and not be at the trailer during the visit with Ruth. Bree had been home a lot more because we had been blessed with a brand-new travel trailer, and we both had a bedroom now. It was much bigger and even had slide-outs. Yet this particular day, I knew that Bree needed to leave even if I didn't understand why. Bree ended up calling her best friend and made arrangements to stay with her. Bree was always welcomed there.

On my way to pick up Ruth, I was able to stop in and visit my dear friends, Aaron and Stanley. They had been a part of my life for close to twenty years. At the time, they were both struggling with addiction. I ended up taking them to lunch and just shared all that had been happening in my life. I'm not sure they knew what to think, but by the end of the visit, I was able to pray for Stanley. I honestly just cried like a baby for them as I drove away. The struggle is very real.

When I pulled in to pick up Ruth at her parents' house, I was a bit excited with anticipation for what the Lord may have planned. I had no idea what to expect or that what was going to happen over the next few days would forever mark and change me. Ruth was excited to spend some time with me and reconnect, as well as to hear what had been happening to me in person rather than just on some short videos I had posted. She loved my truck, and it provided the opportunity to share how the Lord had truly blessed me with it. I had never had a newer vehicle, and I knew that my truck was nothing short of a miracle and blessing and as were so many things in my life at that time and even today.

After our drive to my trailer, Ruth and I got settled in and sat down at my table with our Bibles and began talking. I shared what I was growing in and how our feelings are given to us by God, but they were never given to lead us. I shared that we were lost sons and daughters, but now through the blood of Jesus, we have access to our Father who loves us very much. I explained that healing is for today and that there are many who are stuck in a religious box because they don't have understanding and aren't taught to seek relationship. There was so much I shared about. I had been personally growing with the Lord through His Word. I just didn't question much when it came to scripture. I still believe what my Bible says, and if someone tries to tell me differently, I don't judge them. I just don't embrace what they say. I choose Jesus above all else.

Ruth and I spent hours reading scripture and talking. I was pouring into her everything I had learned about my identity in Christ, which was the opposite of what the world had taught me. I believed I was valuable, but I lived for myself and catered to my flesh most of my life. I allowed feelings to lead a lot of the time, and I didn't exercise any self-discipline when it came to drinking, smoking, or having sex, really anything I wanted. I will say it again: We weren't created to live for ourselves. We have a much greater purpose than to live life to just get what we want and make ourselves happy. Most of the time what we chase doesn't even make us happy. There is repentance and a denying of ourselves before the Lord that we are called to. It is all over the scriptures.

> **Beloved friends, what should be our proper response to God's marvelous mercies? To surrender yourselves to God to be his sacred, living sacrifices. And live in holiness, experiencing all that delights his heart. For this becomes your genuine expression of worship. (Romans 12:1 TPT)**

> **Do you not know that your bodies are temples of the Holy Spirit, who is in you, whom you have received from God? You are not your own; you were bought at a price. Therefore, honor God with your bodies. 1 Corinthians 6:19–20 (NIV)**

> **Then Jesus said to his disciples, "Whoever wants to be my disciple must deny themselves and take up their cross and follow me. For whoever wants to save their life will lose it, but whoever loses their life for me will find it. (Matthew 16:24–25 NIV)**

Ruth seemed to really be embracing and understanding most of what I was sharing. I was able to show her scripture that made it real for her, and it was an amazing evening. Around 1:30 a.m. or so, Ruth said she was tired, and I encouraged her that we had a couple more days so she should get some sleep. I pointed to Bree's room, which was where Ruth was going to sleep, and told her that she had her own room to enjoy. Ruth then stood up and began stretching her back. She mentioned how much her back was hurting her, so I said instantly, "Let's just pray for that, sis."

I stood up and asked her if it was okay if I put my hand on her back, and she agreed that it was no problem. I placed my hand on her back and simply said, "Pain, get out in Jesus name." She looked at me with surprise and said the pain was gone. She then began to share with me about her leg and how she had issues there as well, so I prayed for it. Then she touched her head and shared with me that she had a lump on her head, and she definitely had. It was the size of almost a baseball. She explained that the doctors had run all kinds of tests and put long needles in it, but they didn't know what it was, and it had been there for a couple of years.

Without hesitation, I just laid my hand on the lump; and before I was able to even begin praying, she jerked back and began growling in this deep voice that was not hers. I had no idea what exactly to do, but unafraid, I began shouting, "GET OUT IN JESUS NAME!" I had read in scripture about casting demons out and how we are to have no fear because we have authority through Jesus Christ, but this was something I never thought or imagined I would witness firsthand. I had had a dream about casting a demon out. I had watched it on a couple of videos, but this was right in front of my eyes. This was actually happening inside my home.

For God hath not given us the spirit of fear; but of power, and of love, and of sound mind. (2 Timothy 1:7 KJV)

Heal the sick, cleanse the lepers, raise the dead, cast out devils: freely ye have received, freely give. (Matthew 10:8 KJV)

I had no fear, but I was so caught off guard that all I knew was to say, "Get out in Jesus name." For what seemed like five minutes, Ruth was growling and twisting her body, and then her hands clenched, and she began dropping to the floor. I just kept repeating the same thing. It happened so fast that I didn't have time to think or question anything. I simply believed I had authority because my Bible told me I did. I couldn't tell you how much time passed because it was the last thing on my mind, but as soon as Ruth began slithering like a snake on my floor, I knew I had to stop this thing.

I commanded it and said, "You will stop manifesting in my home, right now!"

Ruth instantly went limp. I stood back silenced. I had no words. I stood there almost like a statue trying to comprehend what just happened. It wasn't long at all that Ruth came to and sat up on the floor and said, "What happened?" I looked at her and said, "Hm, I, ah, I, um, well, I think you may have a demon, sis."

Nonchalantly, she just looked at me and said, "Yeah, I should have told you, but a couple of years ago, this same thing happened." I was lost for words. I was like, *Wait, what?* She began to explain that she had manifested before when others were trying to pray for her, and she ended up tearing her apartment apart, even clawing her walls and so much more. I looked at her completely dumbfounded. I found myself saying, "I have a friend who has dealt with demons. Is it okay if I call her and ask her to come over?"

See, although it wasn't something I had ever seen in person or dealt with, again, I thought of Sally and how she had shared several testimonies about casting out demons. I had believed, but seeing it was totally different from what I had ever imagined or expected. Ruth agreed, and I made a quick phone call. Praise God, Sally was awake and agreed to head straight over.

I'll never forget her walking up to the trailer with such confidence and her Bible tucked under her arm. We talked for a little while, and I shared what Ruth had said to Sally and what had happened. By this time, Ruth was sitting next to me on my little couch, and Sally said, "Zara, I want you to pray so you can understand how to do this."

Without hesitation, I agreed and was fully in. I wasn't afraid, and I knew with all my heart that Jesus was way bigger than any demon. So I reached back behind Ruth's head and placed my hand on the lump, and it happened again. This time, she slid right off the couch and began growling. It was so intense. She almost sounded like Darth Vader, not to be sarcastic; it is just the only way I can explain it.

Sally stepped in and began commanding the spirit to leave. Ruth's hands tightened up again, and her eyes went to the back of her head. At one point, Ruth sat up, and with her teeth clenched together, she began laughing this low evil laugh with blood bubbles appearing through her teeth. I stood back and just said, "Hmm, she's bleeding." Without missing a beat, Sally grabbed Ruth and started singing scripture over her. It was the wildest, most incredible—I would use the word *unbelievable*, but I was there—experience I had ever had happen in front of my eyes.

I can't say exactly how long it took, but it wasn't like hours or anything. When all of a sudden Ruth's body went limp, Sally said, "It's gone." She began inviting Holy Spirit to fill Ruth, and I cannot explain how when Ruth sat up, she looked completely different. It was like an entirely different woman. She was almost glowing. We spent probably twenty minutes on our knees just giving God praise and worship. I knew that I was in and never wanted to do anything else with my life but live for God. Sally later explained to me that demons will do what they can to stay. They will try to cause fear through blood, growling, or whatever. I wasn't sure how to wrap my head around any of it. What I did know was that Ruth was a completely different woman. She was free, and the lump was physically gone. I still speak to Ruth to this day, and that lump never returned.

I literally only made a few videos for Facebook after this, not mentioning this event, because honestly, I just didn't know how to share it with others. I believe that we aren't fighting new demons; these are the same demons that roamed around when Jesus was here. The enemy knows exactly how to come at us and how to try to break us, but I also believe:

Little children, you can be certain that you belong to God and have conquered them, for the One who is living in you is far greater than the one who is in the world. (1 John 4:4 TPT)

Over the next couple of days with Ruth, we spent so much time in the Word. I was simply speechless about how I was talking and looking at a completely different woman. She was one way, and now she was completely different. Jesus changed everything, including her appearance. When I say appearance, there was a darkness to her, and to be honest, there was now a glow to her that was coming from inside her. I can't express how much this time with Ruth changed me. I was never the same and will never be again.

On the way to take Ruth home, I ended up stopping at a bookstore and blessing her with an amazing Bible that she could draw and color in. Ruth is and always has been so talented and creative with her artwork. Now she could do what she loved while in the Lord's Word. Ruth and I decided to start video chats so that we could continue to study and spend time with each other. So we set up a schedule where we would meet once a week over messenger. It was a blessing, and I was simply thankful for all the time we spent.

My friend's uncle, where my trailer was parked, had a beautiful daughter who was a little older than me. Her name is Cindy. Everyone who had known me knew that something huge happened in my life by the way I lived, and I wasn't shy—and still not—to share all God was doing in my life. I may have pulled back from making public videos, but I have never been able to contain my testimony from anyone I meet. How can I after all God has done?

Anyway, Cindy was struggling because her husband was so lost and was taking pills, refusing to work, and pretty much giving her zero support in any way. She asked me if I would mind coming over and praying for him; her love for him was so beautiful and genuine. I agreed, and we made a plan for me to come over to their house so I could pray over him.

I had experienced moments throughout these months where all of a sudden I would be praying for someone and would have a vision or impression in my heart of something random. It was really strange for me. I would just call out what I felt, saw, or heard, and it was always something really important to the person I was praying for. It is still so amazing to me when it happens. When I got to Cindy's house, I walked in and had her husband sit down in a chair while I stood in front of him. I prayed over his health, and then it happened. I began getting really loud, and it was almost as if the Lord took over. I started seeing that the man had given up on life and was trying to kill himself. He had no hope for his future, his wife, or his life. It was so intense how words kept coming out of my mouth as if I had no control. I was just wholeheartedly surrendered to anything the Lord wanted to do, and He did so much in those moments.

Cindy was taken back a bit as was her husband because I began calling things out that he hadn't shared with anyone. I spoke life and prophecy of what the Lord wanted to do with him, and it was one of the most encouraging moments I had experienced.

When I left there, Cindy and her husband were both in tears and overwhelmed by the presence of the Lord as was I. The moment was such a growing experience for me. I never saw Cindy's husband again or talked with Cindy much after this experience, but on the morning of April 17, 2021 (almost three years later), I received this random but so encouraging message from Cindy:

Good morning this is Cindy just thought I would thank you the day you seen my husband the Lord started working on him he's now drug-free and I've been given a second chance with my marriage with him and he thinks you and says that you're an amazing woman which I already knew that LOL just keep on doing what you're doing you're amazing. (Text as sent to me)

ALL GLORY AND PRAISE TO OUR LORD WHO MAKES THE IMPOSSIBLE POSSIBLE!

It was around this same time that I had a wild dream about Dorothy. I woke up without understanding why I would dream something so absurd, but it was so real to me. I convinced myself it was just a silly dream, but it stayed with me, and that was super strange for me. I don't, like I have mentioned, have very many dreams that I remember. I have only had a few that stuck with me, and this was one of them.

I dreamed that Dorothy came to me and wanted to put me in her will. It wasn't just putting me in her will, but she wanted to leave me everything. I didn't fully understand, so I didn't share it with anyone. But about a week later, my heart dropped when Dorothy came to me and said that she made an appointment with her attorney. She said the Lord told her to place me in her will and to leave me everything. I can't express how awkward it was for me because things like this don't really happen, right?

My mother and I were still talking, but our conversations were becoming much shorter. I knew that something was seriously off, but I had been witnessing so much and just believed that anything was possible. I wanted the Lord to heal and restore our relationship so much, yet everything that she would say to me was just discouraging and against what I was seeing, reading, and experiencing in the Lord.

At one point, I really didn't want to take her with us to the Power and Love conference that was coming up in June. However, when I mentioned her maybe not going, she literally said she would hitchhike if she had to. I wasn't going to leave her behind, so I agreed to pick her up when it was time to go. I sold my old rusting truck not long after I was blessed with the "King's Chariot" and put the money up. I was praying about what the Lord wanted me to do with the extra cash and knew my mother had no vehicle. So in prayer, I felt like the Lord was good with me sharing the blessing and helping my mom to get a vehicle.

Now with zero judgment and just simply the truth, my mother has never been very good with money. She spends money as soon as she has it even on things that she doesn't need. Knowing this, it was so important to my heart that she use the money I sent for a vehicle because it was in my heart to help her with that need. So when I called her to tell her I wanted to bless her and get her a vehicle, I explained, "Mom, I just ask that you only use the money for a vehicle because you've been complaining about this, and it's what I want to help with. I feel led to do this for you, so please, tell me that is what you will do with the money."

I was so shocked when she replied to me because, for a couple of months, that was all she would complain about—how she needed a vehicle. Yet her reply was, "I don't want your money or you to help if you're going to tell me how to spend the money you send!"

A lot of things my mother would say to me were challenging my heart so much. I knew who I was in Christ, but it was almost as if she was trying to convince me of the opposite. I couldn't understand how trying to help her turned into me being wrong or demanding. She truly stated that I wasn't helping her if there was a contingency on the help. She told me that if I really wanted to help her with a vehicle, then I just needed to buy her one instead of sending her money for one. It was beginning to affect me in ways I didn't understand. It confused me, and she would often throw the scripture at me:

> **Children, obey your parents in the Lord: for this is right. Honour thy father and mother;**

> **which is the first commandment with promise. (Ephesians 6:1–2 KJV)**

Funny how I didn't just read the scripture and continue with the rest of it myself because I don't believe I would have walked out in confusion about our relationship for as long as I did. The rest of the verse reads:

> **That it may be well with thee, and thou mayest live long on earth. And, ye fathers, provoke not your children to wrath: bring them up in the nurture and admonition of the Lord. (Ephesians 6:3–4 KJV)**

I have a friend that says the King James Version is like the Shakespeare edition, which always makes me giggle. So let's read this in its entirety in the Message:

> ***Children*, do what your parents tell you. This is only right. Honor your father and mother is the first commandment that has a promise attached to it, namely, so you will live well and have a long life. Fathers, don't frustrate your children with no-win scenarios. Take them by the hand and lead them in the way of the Master. (Ephesians 6:1–4 MSG)**

It is important as an adult that we understand this begins with the word *children*. I am not a child; I was once a child, but I am no longer. I spent the next year and a half in a huge struggle trying to honor my mother. It was so challenging because any time I was speaking with her or around her, she would say the worst things. I cannot express how hard it was or how many times I cried out to the Lord to have understanding of how to honor my mother even though she continually caused chaos. In the end, the Lord had to show me that it is praying for her from a heart of forgiveness that I can honor her. This was one of the toughest lessons and fires I have had to walk through. The struggle and war are real. It's not against flesh and blood but against the enemy where those closest to us will be used to attack and challenge us.

> **When I was a child, I talked like a child, I thought like a child, I reasoned like a child. When I became a man, I put the ways of childhood behind me. (1 Corinthians 13:11 NIV)**

I praise the Lord and am beyond thankful that He placed Dorothy in my life. I was able to always go to her and talk to her about the challenges I was facing. She encouraged me to pray for my mother and even stood in prayer with me. It wasn't until the event in June when Dorothy really saw what and why I was so challenged with my relationship with my mom. In the end, my mother refused the help of a vehicle and then gossiped about how wrong I was to anyone who would listen. I just forgave her and kept my heart and eyes focused on Jesus. I continued to pray for restoration and healing in our relationship and held nothing against her. I continue to pray the same to this day even if we do not speak anymore. It is what has had to happen, which I will explain why more in the coming chapters.

I did end up driving up to my mother's house for one night during this month. I can't recall exactly why I went or what I needed to do, but I know I went for something. What I do remember is that my mother and I discussed her will, and she told me she was just going to leave everything with me to distribute to my brothers. I told her I would honor whatever she wanted me to do.

While I was there, my mother also asked me to pray for her brother. I only have two uncles: One molested me when I was younger, and the other raped and beat me when I was in my teens. Here I was, a firm believer in the Lord, and I had zero bitterness or unforgiveness toward either of them. The Lord had already shown me that. If they knew who they were in Christ, neither of them would have touched me. The Lord is so faithful, and even now, those memories are so distant from me that it is as if it wasn't even me who was abused.

My uncle Carl had been diagnosed with cancer, and I was 100 percent willing to lay hands on him and pray that the cancer leave. Love looks like something, right? So I did go to Carl's house and had him jump in my truck. I asked if I could place my hand on his shoulder, and he said yes. I then began to pray for him, and I remember he said something inappropriate, but I didn't care. I just continued to pray for him. I do not know what has happened to the cancer, or if he still suffers from it. What I do know is that, as of this moment, he is still alive. I believe he was given a time frame to live and has currently lived past that time. PRAISE GOD FOR HIS GOODNESS AND FAITHFULNESS!

CHAPTER 8

THE CHALLENGE

June 2018

Still walking and living free from cigarettes, alcohol, pills, weed, and everything, my life was a whirlwind of excitement and travel. I had no desire to go backward and was ready for whatever the Lord wanted to do each and every day. I was seeing so many people around me encouraged and touched just by my simple obedience to living my life for Christ. I was starting to meet with more women throughout the weeks and scheduled appointments just to discuss Jesus.

Dorothy and I were still together almost every day. We shopped together, ate together, and worshipped together. We laughed so much and just enjoyed the fact that we were constantly sharpening each other in the Lord. I loved that all she wanted to talk about was Jesus because He was all that I wanted to talk about as well. There were not many days that we didn't get together. I loved sharing with Dorothy because she would get just as excited as I was. The love we had for each other was nothing short of a miracle and all God. We were complete opposites, and it was so obvious; but through the life I lived, even Dorothy began praying for others whenever she went out.

A couple of the girls who were Bree's friends, from her childhood, were graduating, and I wanted to do something special for them. I took one to buy her a new Bible, and the other wanted to get her nose pierced, so I took her to a tattoo shop. Dorothy came with us, and we had such a moment. It was Dorothy's first time in a tattoo shop, and the tattooist was so nice but had some really bad experiences with some religious people and instantly looked at Dorothy as one of those people. She wasn't, but looking at her, you could see she was almost like a debutante kind of woman. I actually teased her all the time about being a debutante, but she was the kindest person, and there was nothing snobby about her. Not that debutantes are, but let's just say the way the movies portray them is usually snobby.

I was sharing with the tattooist about my testimony and the gospel when all of a sudden, he asked me if I pray for people at Walmart. I just laughed and said, "All the time." He then shared that he thought I had prayed for his wife in the store because she had come home and shared that someone had. He then went on to say that she was actually a Wiccan, so it was odd that I was willing to pray for her.

For some reason, when we are speaking with people, if we find out they are into witchcraft, we instantly act like they are evil. Yet weren't you lost before you turned to the Lord as well? Just something to think about.

The tattooist offered me a great deal for a small tattoo I wanted with what I felt was my "life verse" (a scripture that meant so much to me and had stuck with me since I heard and read it). So while he was tattooing on my arm, "This is how I fight my battles… PRAISE PRAISE PRAISE. Isaiah 61:3." Dorothy and I listened to him share how a *Christian* had told him he was going to hell for having tattoos as he was covered more than I am. It must have affected Dorothy as much as it did me because before we knew it, we were both crying and apologizing to the tattooist, and we reassured him that that isn't who or how Jesus is. He came while we were yet sinners and paid a high price for our sins. He loves us beyond what we could imagine, and He doesn't hold wrongs against us. Love holds no account of wrongs:

> **It [love] does not dishonor others, it is not self-seeking, it is not easily angered, it keeps no record of wrongs. (1 Corinthians 13:5 NIV)**

Love never fails!

We either believe our Bibles, or we don't. We, as believers and followers of Jesus, have to stop picking verses from scripture that fit our agendas and then ignore the other scriptures that we may not agree with. We walk by faith, not perfection, and we are not the judge! We are called, above all else, to love one another. For love moves and motivates a heart to change, not judgment and condemnation. Those are weapons the enemy uses against us.

How quickly we can forget that we were a mess before we turned to Christ. Whether raised in church or just now coming to God, you are His favorite, and He died for you! It isn't our smooth words that move a person's heart; it is Holy Spirit within us that can speak directly to the heart of a person. The choice is and always will be ours individually to believe or not or to follow or not. As His church, we need to stop putting others and God in a box. We aren't all in the same place or have the same understanding or even the same experiences. There is only one truth, but there are so many ways God can reveal that truth—His truth—to each and every one of us. We need to start meeting people where they are rather than expecting them to be where we are.

The tattoo shop experience with Dorothy was something we talked about often. I completely understood where the tattooist was coming from because I have also been rejected because of my tattoos. It is funny because I know my Father sees me through the cross, not my mistakes or my appearance. I'm not saying it will be a tattoo, but scripture does say:

> **On his robe and on his thigh he had inscribed a name: King of Kings and Lord of lords. (Revelation 19:16 TPT)**

> **And he hath on his vesture and on his thigh a name written, King of Kings, And Lord Of Lords. (Revelation 19:16 KJV)**

I'm not claiming it's a tattoo or a body branding. Maybe it's embroidery but sure sounds like a holy mark of some kind!

June 9 was another amazing day. God just blows my mind as each day passes. It was time for our "Café Royal" ladies' night at church, and I was invited to be a guest speaker. I was permitted to set up a book sale stand, and I had a fifteen-minute spot before the main speaker. I did my normal planning for any speaking engagement, which was praying. I don't usually write anything down because I just want Holy Spirit to lead anything that is to be said. I heard Pastor Dan Mohler say one time that the best prayer for a speaking engagement is to ask God, "If it is you in front of these people, Lord, what would you say to them? Please let that be what comes out of my mouth as I speak." That became my prayer before even leaving the house on some days.

It went amazingly well, and I was so blessed to have had the opportunity to share. Then the main speaker came up, and honestly, I just wanted to run up and give her a great big hug. The entire room shifted just as it had before at the other event. It was so apparent that the woman wasn't firm in her identity, and she said some things that I knew were not in line with scripture.

I wasn't spending as much time with Sally, as there were too many things she would say that were so different from what I felt the Lord was showing me in my life. I loved her greatly, and that never changed. Yet here we were again at an event Sally put together, and I knew that the person handed the microphone was not living by the Spirit—not from a place of judgment but by discernment.

Now I am growing as each day passes, but there is something very real with discernment, and we need to pay attention when Holy Spirit is saying, "Warning! Warning!"

There were several things said, and then the speaker began saying that if she could change anything in her life, she would change that her mother and her spouse had passed away. You could instantly feel the bitterness and pain as if it had happened yesterday, yet it had been years.

She discussed a "widows' group" she was a part of, and I knew in my spirit that this was all wrong. We have two choices in the midst of loss. As believers, we can thank God for the amazing time we got with those we love and look forward to an eternity that we will be able to spend with them. Or we can blame God for all the time we feel we are missing with our loved ones, which truly creates bitterness and leaves us open to the enemy. I am not a stranger to the loss of a loved one; however, my perspective of that is no longer a loss but a blessing of the time I was able to spend with that person. I am not disregarding grieving or pain from our losses, but I am encouraging that as believers, we have hope. We are eternal and do not have to allow grief to be the leader of our life in our moments of loss. Yes, walk through the pain but recognize that you do not have to stay there. God wants in on all of that, which means you also don't have to handle it alone.

> **Beloved brothers and sisters, we want you to be quite certain about the truth concerning those who have passed away, so that you won't be overwhelmed with grief like many others who have no hope. (1 Thessalonians 4:13 TPT)**

As I continued to listen to the speaker, I began looking at all of the women sitting there. I knew several of them, and one just happened to be a beautiful sister in Christ who I had been meeting with weekly. Once the event was over, I wanted to go over to the sister I had been discipling to see if she recognized some of the things that were said. I was interested to see if she caught how some things were not lining up with the Word of God, but several women were waiting by my book stand, and I had to go there first.

I praise God for every opportunity He provides for me to share my testimony. I began speaking to and praying for some of the women I was blessed to meet, and it became such an amazing moment. One woman was healed from back issues, and another was blessed and began crying because the presence of the Lord touched her deeply.

When the ladies were done at my book table, I felt blessed to see that my sister and her friend whom she brought to the event were still there. As soon as I was able, I left my table and headed over to where they were.

I smiled at my sister, and she smiled back as I approached. I asked, "So did you hear some of the things we have been discussing?" Things like death and identity in Christ, which ironically, the Lord had been having me work on with my sister.

She smiled really big and said, "Yes, I did."

I wasn't criticizing the speaker, but I knew that the things she was saying were from a hurt platform and not one of hope and victory. As I began talking, I realized that the Lord was leading me to talk about when Paul died. He was my best friend for seventeen years, who passed away from cancer in 2010. I shared how lost I was when that happened. I began sharing how there was peace when I finally realized who I was in Christ. I wasn't sure why I was talking about certain things, and then, as I kept talking, the Lord gave me some words for my sister's friend.

I began speaking words over her about things she was going through in her life, and it was incredible to see her face because Holy Spirit was leading. I had never met the woman, yet there I was saying things that were hitting her heart and were direct to what she was walking through at that time.

It always amazes me when He speaks about someone's life, especially when it is someone who I've never met, because it encourages my faith to know I am listening correctly. I'm not boasting by any means. The Lord is speaking to all of us. The question is, truly, "ARE WE LISTENING?" There is an invitation the Lord has given to each of us, but we have the choice to accept it or not.

So devote yourselves to lavishly supplementing your faith with goodness, and to goodness add understanding, and to understanding add

> **the strength of self-control, and to self-control add patient endurance, and to patient endurance add godliness, and to godliness add mercy toward your brothers and sisters, and to mercy toward others add unending love. Since these virtues are *already* planted deep within, and *you* possess them in *abundant supply*, they will keep you from being inactive or fruitless in your pursuit of knowing Jesus Christ more intimately. But if anyone lacks these things, he is blind, constantly closing his eyes to the mysteries of our faith, and forgetting his innocence—for his past sins have been washed away. For this reason, beloved ones, be eager to confirm and validate that God has *invited you* to salvation and claimed you as his own. If you do these things, you will never stumble. (2 Peter 2:5–10 TPT)**

As I continued to share, my sister ended up looking at her friend and asking, "Have you ever been saved?" My sister's friend responded, saying that she wasn't sure. Our conversation continued for quite a while. Then out of nowhere, I asked her if she had ever felt the Lord's presence, and she said no. I felt led to ask her if she would like to, and she just looked at me and said, "Yes." I then asked permission to place my hand on her. With her permission, I laid my hand on her shoulder and asked Holy Spirit to come to provide her with His wonderful love and peace that only He could so that she knows He is pursuing a relationship with her. After I prayed for her, I looked over and saw she was crying. It was so good. I then asked if she would like to give her life to the Lord, and she said, "Yes." So right then and there, she committed her heart and life to Jesus Christ.

On June 12, it was time for Dorothy and I to load up and head to my mother's house. Bree was driving her own car to meet us there because she had to do some things before heading up. The

Power and Love conference was scheduled to start on June 13–16. I also decided to sign up Dorothy and I as volunteers for the event to just give back and help. We were so excited for the next four days and what the Lord may do.

When we arrived at my mother's house, it was challenging from the moment we walked in. My mother and I have never had a healthy relationship since the time I was born. It was always challenging to even talk to her, but at this time in my life, everything was so different for me. So my heart was for her rather than against her.

As we sat with my mother, she began saying things that left me speechless. At one point, she shared with Dorothy that she was jealous of me because I always did what I wanted and didn't care who I hurt. She also complained about how wrong it was that I wanted to give her money but tell her what to do with it (referring to the car I wanted to help her get). She wasn't hiding these things; she was saying them right in front of me. It was so hurtful, but I realized quickly that I needed to just pray and get alone with the Lord in order to not get upset.

Just because we give our lives to Christ doesn't mean that we never have troubles or that our emotions about things don't still get stirred. Honestly, it's the complete opposite. It is how we handle those trials and fires that shows the rest of the world we are different.

I had to literally walk away at certain times in order to inhale, exhale, and thank the Lord that He was doing work in my life. I knew how changed I was because things that I would have gone off about and gotten very loud in anger over, I couldn't. I didn't react like I used to; I wasn't that person anymore. I was hurting for my mother, and the things she was saying showed that she was truly lost. I realized she was like a puppet on the enemy's strings, and he was using her to attack me. I know she didn't do it on purpose; she just had no idea about the truth and who she was. It got worse as the days went on.

The next morning, we all went to breakfast before hitting the road and heading to Grand Rapids, where the event was being held. We weren't due to check in until the afternoon, so we had a little time. At breakfast, my mother began saying things about my father who I adored. She said she didn't like watching Todd White because he cried, and she felt that a man shouldn't get all emotional like that. She mentioned that it reminded her of my dad and how that drove her crazy because my dad was an emotional man. I simply did all I could to not take it personally.

Dorothy was shocked at the things coming out of my mother's mouth. Dorothy had such a huge heart and couldn't fathom a mother doing or saying the things my mom had in the past or at that time. Her heart was for the Lord to heal my mother and I in our relationship; my heart was and is still for that today. It is truly in God's hands, but we all have independent decisions to make. Just as my uncles would have never hurt or touched me had they understood their value, I believe the same for my mother. I don't believe her intentions are or were to personally hurt me, but she has so much unforgiveness, bitterness, and jealousy that she can't see past herself. It gives the enemy a platform to use her to attack me or anyone else who is close to her.

There were so many moments that Dorothy would look at me, with tears in her eyes, and just whisper, "I'm so sorry, Zara." I was, unfortunately, used to my mother's mouth, but I was changed in how I reacted to it. I had no idea what to do with what was happening inside of me, except to give it to the Lord.

After breakfast, we loaded up and headed out on the open road. What fun we always had just blaring our worship music and praising. Once we arrived at the hotel, we walked up to the front desk to check in. The young man behind the counter didn't have his name tag on, and as I usually do when meeting someone, I asked the Lord, "Father, do you have any words for this person?"

I pray this prayer in my heart, and sometimes, something will come instantly; other times, I don't hear or feel anything.

I smiled and then teased the young man and said, "Where is your name tag, mister?" Without a beat, my mother stepped up and said, "It's in his pocket, Zara. He wants you to get it out for him." I was so humiliated for my mother. How do I even move forward from there? What do I say? "Yeah, we are here to worship and grow as we learn about Jesus, and hey, He loves you"? Nope, I didn't say that because I didn't know what to say.

After that came out of my mom's mouth, all I could do was put my head down and apologize to the young man. I couldn't believe she even said it. Not that sexual comments weren't normal for my mother, but here? Now? I simply kept quiet as I grabbed all our room keys and, again, apologized to the guy as we walked away. Dorothy was so embarrassed she didn't say a word.

Bree did not want to share a room with my mother, so I put her in a connecting room with Dorothy while my mother and I shared a room. We had the door between the rooms open most of the time, which helped me. My mother still watched TV, and I did not, so that took some adjusting for me as well. I wanted to honor her and wasn't going to tell her she couldn't watch television.

When it was time to leave, we loaded up and went to the event center for our meeting for volunteers. They just shared with us their heart and what they needed from us in order to make the event flow as they planned. Dorothy and I ended up working at the welcome table where we checked tickets and gave name badges to those attending. We had so much fun together and met so many different people who were hungry to grow in the Lord. I also had the opportunity, while in Texas, to talk with several of the leaders of Lifestyle Christianity, and they were also in attendance in Michigan. It was so much fun to reconnect with them and just share what had been happening since I last saw them in April.

At this time, Lifestyle Christianity was promoting a new school they were starting up that coming September. It was designed to help equip people in their identity and calling. It wasn't something I felt I was called to at all, but when we arrived, I actually had the thought that perhaps Bree might want to go. I encouraged her to connect with the admissions director who I considered a friend and brother in Christ. After she spoke with him, she said she would pray about it, but she didn't think she was interested.

The first night was amazing, and we all had moments we knew the Lord was speaking directly to our hearts. My mother was beginning to distant herself from us, and perhaps, we were also distancing ourselves from her.

On day two, Bree, Dorothy, and I came together and just prayed for my mom. We weren't sure what to say to her or how to approach her. My mother did ask me to baptize her while we were there, yet something stopped me. I really didn't have an understanding of me baptizing others at this point in my life. I knew we are called to repent and be baptized, but I just didn't feel right baptizing my mom, especially after the things she was saying.

As I reflect on it now, I would have definitely walked her through a repentance talk and dunked her if I had had an understanding. I have grown so much in understanding what baptism is, and it looks nothing like what we see in most churches across America. Over the years, I have had the privilege of baptizing hundreds of people. I have witnessed demons manifest when some of them have come out of that water, and I have firsthand witnessed Holy Spirit filling the heart of a person. I have heard people get out of that water speaking in their prayer language (tongues) and so much more. The scripture doesn't say wait till you can get everyone together on some specific day and then be baptized. Actually, if the heart is being called to repent and be baptized, why wait? I always think about the eunuch that Philip met on the road:

> **The eunuch asked Philip, "Tell me, please, who is the prophet talking about, himself or someone else"? Then Philip began with that very passage of Scripture and told him the good news about Jesus. As they traveled along the road, they came to some water and the eunuch said, "LOOK, HERE IS WATER. WHAT CAN STAND IN THE WAY OF MY BEING BAPTIZED?" And he gave orders to stop the chariot. Then both Philip and the eunuch went down into the water and Philip baptized him. (Acts 8:34–38 NIV)**

> When they heard this they were crushed and realized what they had done to Jesus. Deeply moved, they said to Peter and the other apostles, "What do we need to do, brothers?" Peter replied, "Repent and return to God, and each one of you must be baptized in the name of Jesus, the Anointed One, to have your sins removed. Then you may take hold of the gift of the Holy Spirit." (Acts 2:37–39 TPT)

Baptism is so much more than a scheduled Sunday photo shoot with family all around us. Anyway, I never did baptize my mom, and she ended up pretty mad at me for that. It was as if my mother used every moment we had together to say things against me. I wouldn't respond with anger, and I think that is what the enemy was after. I am not saying my mother is the enemy. Please don't hear that. However, when we allow the enemy access, he will use us against the very kingdom we claim to love. It is through our offense, unforgiveness, or other things we continue to allow in our lives that are not from above that will end up making us his puppets. According to scripture, God is our potter, and we are simply the clay. It takes surrender and will always be our choice:

> Don't you realize that grace frees you to choose your own master? But choose carefully, for you surrender yourself to become a servant-bound to the one you choose to obey. If you choose to love sin, it will become your master, and it will own you and reward you with death. But if you choose to love and obey God, he will lead you into perfect righteousness. (Romans 6:16 TPT)

> One of you will say to me: "Then why does God still blame us? For who is able to resist his will?" But who are you, a human being, to

> **talk back to God? "Shall what is formed say to the one who formed it, 'Why did you make me like this?" Does not the potter have the right to make out of the same lump of clay some pottery for special purposes and some for common use? (Romans 9:19–21 NIV)**

Everything I tried to share with my mother was falling to the ground, and I didn't know what to do or say to her. At one point, when I shared my heart with her about the words she had said to the young man at the check-in desk, she literally looked at me and said, "What are you talking about?" Dumbfounded, I asked Dorothy to come into the room and repeated what my mom said to the young man, and Dorothy looked at my mother and said, "You did say that, honey." My mother sincerely claimed that she didn't remember saying it. It was just the day before, so I instantly knew there was something very demonic going on, but I didn't know what to do about it. My mother couldn't hear or receive from me, so I suggested that perhaps she and Dorothy speak for a while, and I ended up going for a walk. I just prayed for the Lord to step in.

With all that was happening with my mother aside, the event was going amazingly well. Dorothy, Bree, and I were having a blast. Bree ended up meeting Robby Dawkins at one of his book tables, and he was even gracious enough to take a picture with her. Bree was so excited to finally be able to hear him preach live and to get that picture with him.

On the third night, something huge and unexpected happened to Bree. She was in worship and near the front when Holy Spirit made His presence known to her. As she wept, a woman came up to her and said, "You are not an orphan. You are a child of God!" With those words spoken, something broke off of Bree.

I realize you may not know, so I'll share just a little right here. Bree and I went through a seven-year, horrific custody battle with her father and his wife, Jade. Bree was emotionally abused, to say the least. It was really hard for her, and at eleven years old, when the court ordered supervised visitation for her father, he literally walked right out of her life. So the words that the woman said were penetrating to the blame and shame Bree had been carrying around with her. She blamed herself for years for the crazy events that had happened with her father, but it was not her fault at all. That night, she was set free from all of that.

Bree ended up on the floor so overwhelmed by the presence of God and ended up speaking in tongues. She was filled with so much love and had such an amazing moment where the Lord spoke to her. When she stood up, she looked at me with tears rolling down her cheeks and said, "Mom, I am supposed to go to the school. God just told me as clearly as could be."

I just wrapped her in my arms and said, "Okay, baby. He will provide a way if He is calling you to it."

I cannot express how much this moment meant to me or to my daughter. She was confirmed in her identity and knew that she was valuable to the creator of the universe. I cried so much and was so thankful that the Lord was moving in our lives. I had seen some amazing things from healings to deliverances, even being blessed financially more than I could have imagined, but with my daughter realizing she was worthy of the blood of Jesus and valuable to Father, that was something that melted my heart.

Dorothy was so touched and ended up rejoicing with us throughout our entire journey. She was our family; Bree and I had adopted her as our true family, and the bond between the three of us had only grown more and more throughout the years. That was the night Bree realized she did have a Father!

During the last morning, we had to be at the conference an hour before the doors opened to do some volunteer work. Dorothy and I were walking up to the door of the event center together, and there was a huge line that had already gathered. Some were just talking, and others were singing and praising. One guy at the front of the line had a guitar and was playing it while others were worshiping; it was beautiful. Dorothy, with her walker, and I got closer and knew we had to cut through the line to go around the side of the building to the other door where the volunteers entered. I looked at Dorothy as we got closer and said, "Watch this, sis."

She looked at me, and I just grabbed the front of her walker as if to pull on it and yelled really loud, "HURRY UP, WOMAN. YOU ARE SO SLOW!"

Oh, my goodness, you should have seen the people's faces. It was hilarious the way they looked at me. I thought some even looked like they were about to cry. The guy playing guitar even stopped playing and looked at me with the blankest face. They didn't know what to think, and I couldn't hold it back for long. I just busted up laughing. Dorothy died; she hung her head while shaking it and laughing. Oh, it was so funny, and eventually, after a few moments, everyone realized I was joking. That was a moment she and I joked about from that day forward. She would always say to me, "I just can't take you anywhere, Zara."

While Dorothy and I worked the welcome table, we were sitting there one afternoon when a woman came up and said, "Please, can you, ladies, pray for me? I am suffering from a migraine, and I need prayer." Of course, Dorothy and I instantly agreed and placed our hands on the woman. As I started to pray out loud, the woman began to fall on top of our table. I began commanding any unclean spirit to leave and that all pain go with it. It was so incredible; the woman was healed and overwhelmed by the presence of the Lord. We ended up speaking to her for a while, and we connected online. To this day, that woman is a precious gift, and I am thankful the Lord brought us together. We met so many amazing people. One woman I prayed for ended up blessing me with her "spoon ring," which was so sweet.

When I reconnected with some of the leaders of the event, we became even closer as we shared our hearts. My goodness, how I will never forget the blessings and connections we made there. There was another moment when a woman walked up to Dorothy and I. She said, "The Lord showed me that you two are like a ministry team that is meant and works well together. Where one of you stops, the other picks up. I see you two on a carnival ride, like two best friends meant to be together on this ride."

Dorothy and I about started crying because we knew that was from the Lord. There were so many other overwhelming things that happened.

On the final night, Todd White asked if anyone wanted to give their lives to Christ and did an altar call. My mother, even though she had already walked through that with me a couple of months prior, ended up pushing us out of her way to run to the front. I just prayed that the Lord touch her because I had no understanding of why she went. I aimed not to judge her decisions and still pray not to be in judgment of others. Just because I don't understand some things doesn't mean God isn't doing something there. They also did a prayer for anyone who desired to speak in tongues and receive their prayer language; they asked for people to raise their hands. Again, my mother participated. I was so excited for her when it was done. I asked her if she received; she said she did. So I believed that she spoke in tongues and rejoiced for that with her.

Somehow, we all got separated from my mom during the closing of the event. None of us could find her. We had no idea where she had gone, so Bree, Dorothy, and I decided to head to the truck thinking maybe she was there. As we were walking out, there she was, on the floor by the door. Something was really off with her, and she didn't say much of anything the rest of the night. The next morning, after such a wonderful, tough, growing, stretching, and amazing weekend, Bree said she would take my mother home because she knew what had been happening. I had no problem with that plan, and the next thing I knew, Dorothy and I were on the road jamming to our worship music.

We arrived back in Indiana on June 17, and I began looking into Lifestyle Christianity University for Bree. I found that the tuition was doable, but we needed to work out housing for her. As I searched through sites for a rental unit in the Dallas–Fort Worth area, I was shocked at how expensive everything was. I couldn't find a one-bedroom apartment for less than $1,200 a month, and that was far beyond any budget I had. It was so strange because while searching for an apartment, this six-bedroom, three-and-a-half bath, two-car garage, 3,345 square feet ginormous house kept popping up. It was crazy how every time I would search, this particular house always landed in front of me. They were asking like $269,999 for the house, which I confess I laughed at, and thought, *That was absolutely insane.*

As I continued my search, I had thoughts that perhaps once I got Bree settled in her own place, then I would go on the road and do a book tour. Maybe begin to really seek some bookings for speaking events and start pursuing this dream that I hadn't even thought about since January. I mean, I now had a brand-new truck and travel trailer, so I thought, *This might be the time.*

One day, I received a random call from Texas, and I figured it might be one of the properties I was looking at online for Bree. Once I answered the phone, I was completely speechless. It was the real estate agent for the six-bedroom house. I could not, for the life of me, figure out how he got my phone number. I am still not sure to this day other than God had a plan that was not in my hands.

As we spoke, I explained that I had just gotten out of debt, and there was no way I could afford a house like that, but he insisted on taking me through a video walk-through. He kept saying, "Well, let's just see what you think." So to please the man, I scheduled a time to allow him to do a video walk-through with me. When the day arrived, it was wild because he couldn't get his phone to work and kept losing signal in the house. I, of course, shared with Dorothy all that had happened and that is when she looked at me and said, "Zara, I believe the Lord has given me money so I can bring Him glory. I believe this house would do just that."

I had no response except, "Wait, what?" Dorothy went on to explain that she had money and believed the Lord had placed us together for a reason. She said that she wanted to purchase the house for me so that I always had a home, and no one could ever take it away. She said it would be my house, and perhaps, I could provide housing for other students who wanted to attend the school and who were also having a hard time finding affordable living. All I could do was cry and ask her if she was for real. Which, if you ever knew Dorothy, you would know she was very "for real." She wanted to share the blessings she had financially with me and said that we were supposed to do this. It took some time for me to wrap my head around what she was saying, but she encouraged me to look into it. As I did, I realized that I wasn't the only one having a hard time finding housing. I balanced some numbers and realized we could rent out four of the rooms to other students, which would cover the cost to run the house.

I have no words for what I was feeling at that time. I encouraged Dorothy to pray on this, and I would as well. We agreed to stand in agreement for a three-day fast before we made any final decisions. That was really something because Dorothy had never fasted, and for some reason, it was one of my hardest. I was miserable for three days, and so was Dorothy. She had me laughing so hard when she would tell me that she hated fasting and didn't want to do it again all because it made her breath smell, which it does, trust that.

Once the three days were over though, we came together, and we both had so much peace over this decision. I couldn't wrap my head around it; she wanted to pay for the house in full and to have it put in my name. Was this really happening? Dorothy did say that I couldn't go without her, so she wanted to move with me, and I would not have wanted it any other way. At that time, I couldn't have imagined not being near Dorothy to talk and share about each day and all God was doing. So now, the plan was to move to Texas in July—MY MIND WAS BLOWN!

CHAPTER 9

THE BLESSINGS

July 2018

Even today, I can't explain how God did what He did, yet, there I was planning to purchase my first home. I was setting up everything over the phone and had to make all the arrangements for homeowners' insurance and the like. Once everything was in order, the closing was scheduled for July 18. Everything was happening so fast that I could barely keep up. I made arrangements to have my travel trailer stored and found myself packing everything up again. I didn't own much at all and was literally able to put everything I owned into a six-by-twelve U-Haul trailer.

Dorothy was preparing for the move as well. She kept suggesting that she sell her home in Indiana, but something inside of me did not think that was a good idea. So we both agreed that we would wait to make that decision. Dorothy ended up putting me in charge of all of her finances, and I prayed so much about that because I never wanted her to feel like I would take advantage. More importantly, I knew my heart. I wanted to honor Dorothy and knew that responsibility was something I never imagined, and I didn't want to do anything wrong. I had never had access to so much money, but I knew that God was doing something here, so fear was never an issue for me. I would just pray about everything before making any decision, and, of course, Dorothy and I would discuss any purchases.

I had many thoughts about what others must think. I knew that Dorothy was well-known, and everyone looked at her as this older woman, but I am telling you—she was so young at heart it was amazing. I was concerned that others would think I was taking advantage somehow, but I would kick those thoughts straight to the feet of Jesus. I knew that this was all Father, and so did Dorothy, so what could anyone say against it?

I had a couple of meetings with her and a few of her friends who wanted to meet me throughout the months. It always amazed me how they would tell me that the Lord already revealed to them that He was the one putting us together. It was such a confirmation for both Dorothy and me. Before we moved, Dorothy had one friend who wanted to sit with me and talk, so we made arrangements and met at the local coffee house. I was always open to meeting any of her friends. I just admired Dorothy so much.

The day came for our meeting, and Dorothy and I walked into the coffee house full of energy; we usually were though. When her friend arrived, she didn't waste any time at all. She looked right at me and said, "When Dorothy told me she was moving to Texas with you, I have to be honest. It bothered me a lot. Once I sat down and began praying over this though, the Lord showed me that this is His calling and that He wants her to move with you."

I can't express how much things like this gave me so much peace about the decisions we were making. I was overwhelmed by all of it, and it seemed like a dream, yet there I was—living it.

I did a lot of research and began posting housing opportunities for some of my rooms on the Lifestyle Christianity housing page. It wasn't long until I began receiving responses from other ladies who were looking for a place to stay during the first three-month semester. I was so excited because everything was coming together. I made the rooms super cheap compared to everything I had researched in the area. My intention was not to make things hard for anyone but to still support the monthly bills for the house. Yup, I also made it a "women-only" house.

I started putting together a plan for how to house everyone and what I would charge for rent. I put together a rental contract, a plan to get furniture once we arrived in Texas, and all that I could possibly think of that would make a bunch of strangers living together go smoothly. My heart was to dedicate the house to the Lord and just do whatever He wanted. Dorothy didn't mind anything I came up with; she supported all of my ideas and encouraged me to keep in prayer before finalizing anything.

One night, Dorothy and I were sitting together when this text came through on my phone (note: neither of us knew the young lady who sent it):

> *Hey, Zara, I'm not attending LCU until fall 2019, but I would just like to thank you for your obedience in the Lord and seeking him out with the house. You have provided a refuge and "house of God" for young women growing in the Lord to live in. That house will be filled with nights of worship, healthy confrontations (the iron sharpens iron type), confessions, shared meals…that house will help foster a spiritual family, all because you were faithful to step out. So thank you. Even if I never get to use or even see it, it has inspired and encouraged me.*

As I read this out loud, I began crying. I couldn't believe we hadn't even been to the house or even finalized the closing, but God was using others to encourage us that we were making the right move. Another random message came through that said:

> *Hey, Zara, I'm gonna be honest… I don't regularly prophesy, so I won't say "the Lord says," but what I'm going to tell you is what I feel in my heart when I see your picture: I feel like you're God's peculiar treasure, He loves to see you smile, and I feel like your joy is the strength God has given you for God is your strength. He is the one making all things*

work together for good to you because He has seen and sees your love and passion for Him. I feel like your smile shines so bright that it overshadows all the scars from the past, but at the same time those scars are like an epistle read in all the spiritual realm, the marks you bear are the signs of battles you fought...you are delicate as the Father's child but you are also a warrior. Keep on fighting the good fight of faith; yours is the victory. God is with you; you are greatly beloved. God bless you mightily! From Argentina.

I can't explain how or why about a lot of things as I have said now a few times, but these kinds of messages came in and just brought me to tears. I felt like the Lord was reaching out to me and confirming for me that my doubts weren't Him. I was nervous, yes. I had just lived a whirlwind life that I had never known for close to six months, and now, now I am purchasing my first home and providing housing for others as well. I didn't even see it as my house; it was His house.

Dorothy and I were all packed up, and Bree was going to drive down a couple of weeks later because she had a concert that she wanted to attend with her best friend. I researched the area and prices and made sure that Dorothy and I arrived in Texas the day before the closing in order to arrange for furniture and appliances to be delivered in the afternoon of the 18. It was simply a miracle the way everything came together. Before getting on the road, we stopped by the bank, and I was literally handed a $241,118.45 cashier's check, which was the cash purchase amount agreed on for the house. Talk about mind-blowing. With everything I had been experiencing, then this. Yeah, I'm still speechless about how all of this came together!

There we were, loaded in the beautiful King's Chariot and headed to Texas to live. That was the last state or place I ever imagined I would be moving to, but I was on my way with my best friend right next to me.

> **Trust in the Lord and do good; dwell in the land and enjoy safe pasture. Take delight in the Lord, and he will give you the desires of your heart. Commit your way to the Lord; trust in him and he will do this: He will make your righteous reward shine like the dawn, your vindication like the noonday sun. (Psalm 37:3–6 NIV)**

I tried to share with friends what was happening to me, but many people believed that I was making money from my book. I don't think many people, even now, realize my book didn't go anywhere during this time. A lot of people thought I was just successful, but truth is, my success has come from God. I would call it blessings rather than success though. I literally just set aside anything to do with my book and would only even think about it on occasion. I knew that God led me to write my other book, but at this time in my life, I was right where I was supposed to be. So I continue to live my life surrendered and believe that everything is in His hands as I continue to follow His lead. Suppose we shall see what He does next because following Him is one ride I never want off of. One minute, you'll think you are going one way, and the next, He says, "Nope, not yet." It is actually so much fun, but it is definitely not without its trials, fires, and tests.

We arrived in Texas on the seventeenth and got to the furniture store in time to put in our order for the furniture that I picked out. We had a lot of space to fill; it was a 3,345-square-foot home, and we had a six-by-twelve trailer of things, and that was it. I decided that the four rooms I was going to rent out would be the renters' responsibility to fill. I wasn't going to purchase things for the ladies renting my rooms because I felt that would be silly to do. They could be responsible for their own beds and whatever else they wanted because they would be with us for only three months unless they stayed for another semester and didn't decide to go home or somewhere else. Most of the ladies I agreed to rent to were from out of state and just coming for school, not to move to Texas. I had five ladies set to move in early September. Two of the girls were going to be roommates, and the other three had their own rooms.

Everything I picked out to have delivered was with everyone in mind that Father may bring to the house. I grabbed two sectional couches, an eight-person dining room table, two refrigerators (one for us and one for the ladies renting), a washer and dryer, and a few other items we needed. I also grabbed three-bedroom sets for Bree, Dorothy, and I. Everything was set to be delivered the next day, on the eighteenth, at noon. I was praying that was enough time for the closing with Dorothy and I being able to get over to the new house in time.

We had two living rooms in the house, so I made sure to find a beautiful living room set for the upstairs as well. There were two bathrooms upstairs and five bedrooms plus the living room. Then downstairs, there was a massively huge master bedroom with the master bathroom plus a half bathroom off the foyer. We had a living room, kitchen, dining room, foyer, and laundry room, not to mention the two-car garage. I had spent a lot of time looking through all the pictures of the house online and had a vision of how I was going to put the house together before we ever stepped inside. Bree would have her own room upstairs, and Dorothy and I planned to share the huge room downstairs, giving the other four rooms to help other students. I was feeling nervous but so giddy like a little kid with anticipation.

This was also six months to the day when I had an encounter with Holy Spirit and was set on fire. My entire life drastically changed on January 17, 2018. It was four days later that I threw out my cigarettes, weed, alcohol, and pills. See, for me, my experience wasn't that I cleaned up and then came to God. It wasn't that I had to change everything, and then He showed up. I literally was seeking Him in the midst of my mess, and He came to overwhelm me and cover me with His love. He showed me that I was valuable and that I was His daughter. He changed me from within, not by my works!

Did I want to change? Yes, I wanted change, but I can honestly say that it was after He touched my heart that I desired to obey Him. I wanted to know Him more. That was what allowed His love to penetrate me, my desire to know Him. I was seeking with a pure heart, not a perfect life. It was my willingness to let go of all the yuck, hurt, abuse, and unforgiveness that I had held onto. I invited Him into all of it. I know churches that won't even baptize a crying heart if the person is living in sin; that alone floors me. Being His means that you shine His light and shift atmospheres, but more importantly, it means you personally have a relationship with Him, not just listen to your favorite preacher once or twice a week. We are called to be disciples and make disciples—to produce good fruit so that others may eat off of our lives and see that God is good. When we come with judgment or actually believe that being His has to look a certain way, I'm afraid we are already missing it!

God can do anything to anyone. He will not, however, force Himself on you. He wants us to choose Him, to choose to follow Him. I always wondered why He even put the Tree of Knowledge of Good and Evil in the garden. Then I realized that He wanted Adam and Eve to choose to listen just as He does for us today. We ask the question, "Why?" all the time rather than just saying, "Lord, you have a better way, a better plan, and I trust you." Why is there so much evil in the world? Why do babies die or those we love? Why do our loved ones get cancer? Why, why, why? Yet, we are missing the fact that we are in a fallen world, and the enemy is just as real as Father is. The enemy comes to kill, steal, and destroy. The reason Jesus hasn't returned is to give us more time as the church to reach the lost. Come on, God wants everyone to turn to Him, but some accept and believe, and others do not. Yet He pursues them and calls us as His children to live a life that glorifies Him so that others may see His goodness. There are four grounds found in Mark 4:

The farmer plants seed by taking God's word to others. The seed that fell on the footpath

> represents those who hear the message, only to have Satan come at once and take it away. The seed on the rocky soil represents those who hear the message and immediately receive it with joy. But since they don't have deep roots, they don't last long. They fall away as soon as they have problems or are persecuted for believing God's word. The seed that fell among the thorns represents others who hear God's word, but all too quickly the message is crowded out by the worries of this life, the lure of wealth, and the desire for other things, so no fruit is produced. And the seed that fell on good soil represents those who hear and accept God's word and produce a harvest of thirty, sixty, or even a hundred times as much as had been planted! (Mark 4:14–20 NLT)

Holy Spirit is the best teacher, guide, and comforter. We have to remember it is a relationship, and no relationship looks the same. Maybe there are some similarities, but being like-minded doesn't mean we are the exact same. When you are alone, are you seeking Him? When no one is looking, are you talking to Him? Do you worship when no one is looking? Do you give your time more to complaining at Him or thanking Him? Do you spend more time watching TV than you ever spend in your Bible? What lyrics are you singing over yourself? Oh, that's a big one for me. Have you really paid attention to the songs you are listening to, filling yourself with, and singing over yourself?

These are the simple things that can change everything. It is what we do in our alone time that matters. He knows our hearts. He sees you at all times, not just when you attend church on Sunday. Most religious people act like He's afraid to be in the bar with the lost. Yet Jesus ate with the sinners, the lost, the broken. He isn't afraid that someone's sin will get on Him, so why are we? If we are covered in His blood and washed clean, called to be a light, why are some of us actually afraid of the dark? Darkness is literally the absence of light, so darkness wouldn't be the issue; it would be the absence of light that is the issue, right?

He sees you. He knows you, but if you don't seek Him, you will miss the beauty of knowing Him. The excitement of encountering His goodness and mercy will only be sitting there waiting for you—waiting for you to believe and choose to accept that it is really available to you. Not believing He loves you doesn't and will never change the fact that He truly loves you. Your unbelief will never change the truth!

> **When you pray, don't be like the hypocrites who love to pray publicly on street corners and in the synagogues where everyone can see them. I tell you the truth, that is all the reward they will ever get. But when you pray, go away by yourself, shut the door behind you, and pray to your Father in private. Then your Father, who see everything, will reward you. (Matthew 6:5–6 NLT)**

This doesn't mean that we don't pray for those in need. This means what are you doing with your alone time? I think *The Chosen* series is one of the best shows I've ever given my time to watch. There is a line in it where the actress that plays Mary Magdalene says, "I was one way, and now I am completely different, and the thing that happened in between was Him!" I just can't express how much that one statement was exactly how my heart felt. How my life lived was and is the very expression of this one statement.

If you haven't seen the series, I just can't encourage you enough to go check it out. It is incredible and will bless you beyond measure. It is unlike any show about Jesus and His disciples that you will ever watch, in my opinion! So that it is clear, I am not being paid or does anyone from *The Chosen* know I am writing this right now. This isn't some promotion; this is how I feel and what I personally believe. I, literally, have introduced so many people to this show, including purchasing DVDs just to bless others with it. So please don't think I am promoting anything here. I am the same way in person.

Now the morning of the eighteenth arrived. Dorothy and I got up and got all our things together and headed to the office for the closing of the house. It all went so smoothly that it was almost surreal. Yes, I purchased the house before even stepping inside of it. Crazy you say? Well, how could I not when I knew with all my heart that it was God who put it all together? I knew that I knew what I knew! The way it all came together was supernatural from the day the house began appearing on my laptop to the day the real estate agent called me. I had so much peace and so many confirmations that I didn't need to see it. I just trusted the Lord and walked by faith.

Once all the paperwork was signed, cashier check exchanged, and hands shaken, I was handed the keys to my first home. I'm not sure I can express the emotions that I felt because the excitement of what God had planned was so tremendous. I knew that He had me, and the fact that Dorothy was right there with me, walking through the entire process, brought me so much joy. I was able to share every step of the adventure with someone who loved me and wanted to be there to support me. I was and am so beyond blessed.

We got to the house with about an hour and a half to spare before all of the furniture was scheduled to arrive. I put the key in the door and was taken back by how truly huge and beautiful the house was. From the moment we walked into the house, Dorothy and I began praying over the home. We prayed and invited the Lord to make that house His own. We invited Holy Spirit to consume the house and do with it whatever He wanted. As I walked around, I cried as I prayed and knew that this was an impossible event that God made possible. I asked the Lord to cover the house from the top of the roof to the very foundation. I walked room to room, simply blessing and praying over who may come to the house and whoever may stay at the house and that the Lord lead all that was going to happen in the house. It was so comforting, and there was this amazing feeling of peace over my home.

The delivery guys showed up on time, and the process of putting the house together began. At one point, one of the guys putting my couches together asked me, "Have you ever been to Upper Room?"

With a big smile, I was able to say, "Yes, I actually have."

He then proceeded to say, "This house feels like it does there. I feel the presence of the Lord in this house."

My heart literally jumped with joy. It was a beautiful opportunity to share my testimony with the man. He was a believer and loved the Lord a great deal, so the entire thing encouraged his faith even more.

That was it, my heart's desire was and is that anyone who comes into my home feels the Lord's presence—His peace. Over the next few weeks, I spent every moment building and putting together a home that would be welcoming and sufficient for anyone who would come to stay or visit. I ended up building a gym in the garage and placed one of the refrigerators in there for the ladies who would be renting rooms. I put shelves together so everyone would have their own personally space for their food; the bathrooms were set up for sharing with their own small drawers. I marked each room with letters so that everyone knew whose space was whose. I did all I could to bless and make things as easy for whoever the Lord wanted to bring into the home.

I purposely did not hang many personal pictures because I just didn't feel like this was specifically "my home"; this was the Lord's house. So I ended up getting a lot of pictures with scripture and even made creative writings on the walls with the Lord's words. I turned one of the walls in the laundry room into an art wall, where I planned to allow anyone who stayed at the house to paint anything they wanted. It was all coming together, and I was so thankful Dorothy was there.

Although Dorothy wasn't physically able to do too much, she was such a blessing. She would read scripture to me while I would paint and work on the house. Our conversations were never dull. I would ask questions about scripture or life, and she would always say, "You ask the best questions, Zara," and then she would show me or read to me in the Bible what God had to say about the topic. I loved my time with Dorothy. For months, it was really just her and I for hours on end. We never ran out of things to talk about. She always made me laugh because she would say things like, "You amaze me, Zara. I've never met a woman who can do everything. I don't think there is anything you can't do." It impressed her how the house was coming together and how I designed and set things up. For me, it wasn't that big of a deal, but she just thought it was so cool and something special.

I ended up making one bathroom upstairs a red room, and the other was a blue room (the colors I decorated with). I was just trying to make everything as easy for others as possible. I ended up putting everything together as far as rules for the house and a contract for renting a room, and I came up with a plan to have "family meetings" with all the girls so we could all get to know one another more.

I was so stoked to meet all the ladies who were scheduled to rent the rooms. I had prayed over each and every one of them and knew that this was going to be a new adventure. There were five new strangers coming into the house to share in the blessings. I was so open to the new relationships that would come from our time together. I felt like the Lord was going to place people in my life who would be sisters, and the love between us would be knitted together by our Father.

I can't express how I was so overwhelmed by all that was happening so fast. Everything was ready by the end of the month. I could barely even sit still because of my excitement. My brother, Dakota, would call here and there; we never lost touch, and I think once he started seeing that this was who I was, he began to believe God was really doing something.

I'm not sure Dakota knew what to think, but all I kept telling him was that this was all God. It was so important to my heart that when he or anyone else looked at the blessings I was given, they see Father in it. I didn't want to point to the person or persons who had blessed me. Truth is, anyone who has blessed me didn't want recognition, including Dorothy. It was always discussed that it was

God who was in charge and should get the glory. I never, not one time, asked for anything, but God provided beyond what I could have ever imagined.

For some people, all they could see was someone else or the person who was helping me rather than Father who led the person. The truth is, that is how God works. He doesn't just make money appear in our bank accounts or in a duffel bag in the living room when we wake up. He uses others to bless others. He calls us to help one another.

The problem a lot of us have is that we tend to block our blessings with our pride or false humility. If I had stayed in the mindset that I need to work for all I want and can't accept a gift from anyone and if I would have stayed in my pride, I don't know where I would be today. I am not saying we shouldn't work, but we need to be open to receiving and giving. We need to realize that God is a good Father and a good provider, but we have a role to play in that. Whether He has blessed you to give or whether He has blessed you by having another give to you, don't allow your pride to say you can't accept or afford to do what He tells you.

> **God's marvelous grace imparts to each one of us varying gifts. So if God has given you the grace-gift of prophesy, activate your gift by using the proportion of faith you have to prophesy. If your grace-gift is serving, then thrive in serving others well. If you have the grace-gift of encouragement, then use it often to encourage others. If you have the grace-gift of giving to meet the needs of others, then may you prosper in your generosity without any fanfare. If you have the gift of leadership, be passionate about your leadership. And if you have the gift of showing compassion, then flourish in your cheerful display of compassion. (Romans 12:6–8 TPT)**

Honestly, I would encourage you to get in your Bible and continue to read this entire chapter. If you do that, I would even encourage you to read the entire book of Romans and just hit the rest of your Bible while you are there. It is so incredible how much the Word comes to life when we allow it to penetrate our hearts and not just read it like a book or only listen when a preacher reads it, especially when we read it and invite the Lord into the time we are reading because then it becomes more than just words. I have literally met people who know the Bible extremely well but don't have a clue as to who God is and how much He loves them. It's easy to remember or quote scripture, but allowing it to become real to your heart is a whole other story. It is the living Word of God, and it has the power to shake walls down, break chains, and change lives, but it all starts with having faith and believing:

> **So search your hearts every day, my brothers and sisters, and make sure that none of you has evil or unbelief hiding within you. For it will lead you astray, and make you unresponsive to the living God. (Hebrews 3:12 TPT)**

> **Now faith is confidence in what we hope for and assurance about what we do not see. (Hebrews 11:1 NIV)**

As July was coming to an end, the house was pretty much put together and ready for anything the Lord wanted to do. Dorothy and I were scheduled to head to Las Vegas for another event called "Holy Spirit Conference," but because of all the work and the travel we had been doing, we decided it was best to cancel the trip. My mother had also decided that even though I had paid my phone bill, which was on her account at the time, she wanted me to get off of her plan. I wasn't to upset about it, but I was a bit surprised. I knew she was angry because of all that had been happening to me. She was extremely jealous because of my blessings, but I continued to just try to love her through it.

I went up to the phone company and found out she hadn't been paying the bill at all, not even with the money I sent her. In order to be removed from her account, I had to pay the bill in full. I was a little upset at how she tricked me, and I believe she did it intentionally, but I went ahead and paid her bill in full and got set up on my own account. It was really hard because I didn't know how to continue being in a relationship with her when she was continually trying to bring confusion and chaos into my life.

CHAPTER 10

THE WORK

August 2018

Now I have walked through a lot in my lifetime. From being molested, beaten, raped, addiction, living in a tent—well, you name it—I have probably walked through it. Over the next few months, there came lessons, fires, and stretching that I never saw coming. I just knew that Jesus was amazing. Father loves us, and He changed everything in my life. Up to this point, I had witnessed and walked through things that I could have never even imagined I would have. Yet there was so much more to grow in and come to understand. The next few months brought a lot to me that did just that—grew me and helped me become the woman I am today.

Dorothy and I were scheduled to travel back to Indiana for a concert that Dorothy had to be at. She was a singer in a group in her youth, and they were having a reunion that she needed to be in attendance. There came a point that she shared with me that she didn't share friends well. She had a hard time when she would have a friend throughout her life because she wanted that friend all to herself. I thought it was odd because she was so loved and had many friends, but she meant that one best friend. She shared with me that the Lord had to work on her heart on that, and she was still growing every day. I always found it so encouraging to know her. She was always excited about what the Lord was doing, and she had no hard feelings about not knowing things. I mean, she loved the new things that were happening and held no regrets. Instead of seeing it as if she had been missing out, she was just thankful to be in the now.

Bree arrived at the new house and was taken back by how big it was. Every day, Bree was growing more and more into the woman of God she was always called to be. It was so precious, and I was so grateful to see what the Lord was doing in my daughter's life. When Dorothy and I had to go back to Indiana for the concert, we left Bree at the house for the week. It was hilarious because I told her I had the security cameras up, but she couldn't see them. I actually hadn't had the chance to get any cameras up yet, except for the front porch. I had no idea that for the entire week, she would be talking to me through the vents thinking there were cameras in them. I still can't help but laugh so hard when I think about it. She literally asked me when I got back if I heard her say good morning and talk to me while I was gone. By that time, I had forgotten that I teased her, so I asked her what she meant. She explained that she thought the cameras were in the vents and had been talking to me through them all week. Oh, my goodness, Dorothy and I died laughing. Bree was mad, not in a mean way. She just said, "Really, Mom, really?" Man, that still makes me laugh to tears because I could so see Bree talking to the vents.

As I continued to pray and spend time with the Lord, I felt like He was calling me to hold gatherings at the house for other students, not just the ones who would be living with us. I ended up posting that we would be holding Bible studies and inviting any students who would like to join us. I knew that I was where the Lord had called me, and it was important to my heart to abide in all He called me to. I am a firm believer that when the Lord calls us to something, He will provide all we need to get through it. I felt that this was no different. Although most of the time, as I've come to learn, it is outside of our comfort zone, many of us want to be sent and do for the Lord, but we only want to go when He provides what we need. I've learned that most of the time, He will call us to something and provide all we need as we go as we step out in faith and trust in His provision.

During the month, my friend who had called me in April, the one who wanted to order books for the work release program, got ahold of me. The woman he was running the program with, Jezzy, wanted to meet me, and I planned to fly up to Pennsylvania to meet with her, but the travel plans got canceled. In the end, I booked a flight for her to come down to me in September. I began being connected with a lot of people, and I loved it.

My sister in Christ, Esther, the one who annoyed me when I was placed next to her at the event in April, ended up getting ahold of me as well. She was so excited when I told her that God had provided me with a home in Texas, and I was now living there. Esther instantly said, "I'm sorry, Zara. That's on me because I asked God to bring more godly women around me, and I believe He answered my prayers by brining you here."

It definitely made me laugh, and I said, "Oh, so it's your fault I'm here. I see."

It is so ironic when we first meet people and think that we could never be friends, yet God has much bigger plans than we realize.

I began seeing Esther a lot; she came to the house often and visited. We were both good for each other. Where I lacked in certain understanding, she helped; and where she lacked, I helped her. Dorothy absolutely loved Esther as well. It was such a God-given friendship among the three of us. We all spent time in the Word together and sharpening one another. We even went over to spend time with Esther's mother and stepfather, which was an absolute blessing.

At one point, throughout the year, I just gave up on my weight. I didn't care what my body looked like because I was more interested in my spiritual growth. It was not good because the truth is, we are made of three parts: body, soul, and spirit. We are actually called to steward all three. For me, I used to be so caught up in my appearance and weight that I just laid it all down. I had no interest in trying to lose weight as I had in the past. I did end up gaining quite a bit and was as big as I was when Bree was born. It bothered me in some ways, but I felt like my spiritual growth was way more important. When I built the gym in the garage, I was sure I would get back on track, but the truth is, I never did. I even had a friend use the scripture:

> **For bodily exercise profiteth little: but godliness is profitable unto all things, having promise of the life that now is, and of that which is to come. (1 Timothy 4:8 KJV)**

I think it was to encourage me that my weight wasn't a big deal, but truth is, we need to take care of ourselves—not only spiritually but also physically and mentally. We need to recognize that it is important to honor the bodies God has given us and stop using the excuse, "He's going to give us new bodies anyway." Perhaps I am writing this for just me, but I sometimes need the reminder that God cares about all the details, and this life is short. If we have gluttony for food, we have a problem that we sincerely need to pray on. If we are addicted to anything and have a view of, "I can't live without it," we have a problem. The cool thing is that we have an answer too. There are so many resources to help us, and God has given us self-control. We just need to get in line with our Father and stay focused on the things above, which will help us lose focus on what we were never created for, to begin with. Easy? NOPE, BUT WORTH IT! My heart was rocked when I read the scripture that says:

> **Consider him who endured such opposition from sinners, so that you will not grow weary and lose heart. In your struggle against sin, you have not yet resisted to the point of shedding your blood. (Hebrews 12:3–4 NIV)**

That verse pierced my heart and still does. My goodness, how quickly we grow weary when challenges come or when we focus on ourselves. We are called to keep our eyes on Him. I have discovered and been guilty of using what someone has done against me or circumstances or just wrong thinking to be my justification to sin. It took me a long time to understand that those things are just momentary, and the price Jesus paid for me is much greater. He made the sacrifice so that I can overcome and not look at what's happening but rather look at what He has done. It isn't easy to walk it out, but I can honestly say it gets easier as we keep our eyes on Him. As we draw nearer and get His Word in our hearts, we grow to an understanding of what He says rather than what we feel or see. It is important that we get in line with Him, and that includes taking care of ourselves. He says:

Love the Lord your God with all your heart and with all your soul and with all your strength. The second is this: Love your neighbor as yourself. There is no commandment greater than these. (Mark 12:30–31 NIV)

I'm still growing in understanding of how to love myself as Father calls me to. As life went on, Dorothy and I went everywhere together. It was very rare that I wasn't loading Dorothy up to roll with me if I left the house. She loved seeing me in stores because I simply couldn't contain talking with people and sharing my heart. I prayed for many people no matter where I was. I also confess that I loved and still love praying for people, but there was a thought that was coming in that Dorothy was only with me to see the miracles and healings that were happening. At one point, I asked her that if I stopped praying for people, would she still want to be around me? With tears in her eyes, she told me she loved me, and it wasn't about that for her. She admitted though that she didn't want me to go anywhere without her because my life was exciting, and she loved watching me and the way I lived.

I also reconnected with some people who I grew up with in New Mexico. I hadn't seen or spoken with most of them, except for my one friend who reached out in April, in over twenty-five years. We all followed each other on Facebook, and when they saw I had moved to Texas, we all planned a barbecue at my house. We set it up for September 3, so I had a lot to get ready for. I went ahead and purchased a grill, and what was said to take three hours to put together took me six, but I got that darn thing together.

By the end of the month, everything was ready, including security cameras. I installed a lock on the door that had a keypad, so anyone who lived there had their own code. I placed security cameras downstairs and one in the living room upstairs. My thought was that it would give the ladies extra comfort to know that there was security. I also changed all the door handles in the bedrooms so that the ladies could lock their own doors and have their own keys to their rooms.

Dorothy, Bree, and I had an event that was scheduled for September 5–9 in San Antonio, Texas, with Bill Johnson, Randy Clark, and Robby Dawkins—plus a few other speakers. We made plans to go to the event months in advance, but it was becoming challenging as well because the ladies were all scheduled to arrive around that time. Jezzy was scheduled to fly in from Pennsylvania on the third, the same day my childhood friends were coming. It was also the day two of the ladies were supposed to move in. The plan was to just take Jezzy to the conference with us. Needless to say, preparing for September was a bit hectic, but I trusted the Lord would work it all out.

CHAPTER 11

THE START

September 2018

It seemed like time was flying. I couldn't believe that the house was about to be filled. I had all paperwork, house rules, keys, and everything ready for each of the ladies so that when they arrived, I would be able to walk them through and show them their rooms and areas for food and so forth. I had no idea what I was doing, but looking from the outside, it looked like I did. I was just giving everything my all. Some of the ladies had already shipped things to the house, and I just placed their boxes in their rooms.

Jewel was the first to arrive. She came in from Georgia with her mom, and it was such a blessing to meet them both. I knew from the moment I met Jewel that she was special. I also knew that there was something following her around, and after talking with her mom, it was confirmed that Jewel came to be set free and grow.

Jewel was so quiet and shy. She had the sweetest voice, but you could barely hear her because she spoke so quietly. I was excited to have her at the house, and she truly blessed me by just being there. Jewel was in her early twenties, and her mom was super precious. I walked them through the paperwork and then showed them the house. Jewel ended up having a bed and other things delivered to the house as she needed. She had suffered from scoliosis in her youth, and most of her back was metal so she had some issues, but she was a fighter. She was so passive, and I cannot express again how quiet she was. I loved her from the moment I met her. Her mother and I clicked right away as well, and we got along from the start. I loved the fact that they were so open to being there, and that Jewel was hungry for understanding her identity.

On September 3, I sent Bree to the airport to pick up Jezzy, my friends from New Mexico came for a barbecue, and two of the other girls arrived. My friends showed up first and filled the house up. It was awesome. They brought food and cooked an authentic delicious Mexican lunch. I got to visit with three of the six kids in the same family that I had grown up with in Las Cruces. I always referred to them as the "Butterfield Gang" because that is where we all met as kids—Butterfield Park.

I'm not sure they knew what to think of my testimony and how I ended up there, but they listened, and we all shared stories and where we were in our lives. I was blessed with the privilege to pray for my friend's husband. Although we didn't see a healing, it was an honor that he allowed me to pray. I can't explain why everyone doesn't get healed. All I know is stepping out in faith is a calling we all have. It is not up to us to do the healing, but it is up to us to have faith and step out. One thing I do know is that there is not one prayer that is not heard. Whether something happens the way we want it to or think it should or not, God hears us.

If I recall correctly, Suzy showed up first. Suzy was a beautiful nineteen-year-old young lady from Texas. She was so full of life. Her smile was dynamic, and she loved the Lord a great deal. Her heart was to be a wife and mother, which I could relate to at that age. She had already met a man and felt he was the one God told her to marry. At this time, I had zero understanding of dating and what that looked like with the Lord leading, so I just stayed away from it and tried not to share too much. Although I had my moments, my heart was more like, "Don't date. Let God lead everything," but that was me. Suzy was in a totally different place. She had such a heart full of love and wanted to share it with someone. She was a little shy, but that soon broke off as each day passed. Suzy had attended Bethel School of Ministry and had been kicked out due to some intimacy that was against the rules. She was ready for a fresh start and wanted so badly to stay focused and not fall backward. Her mother was super charismatic and a very different kind of woman. I had never met anyone quite like her; she was what I guess you could call *super spiritual.*

Next to arrive at the house was Karen who drove in from Wyoming. Now Karen was the youngest to join the house. She was almost eighteen years old, and yet, she was the biggest girl in the house in height and size. She was loud and extremely opposite from the other two girls. Her laugh was so contagious, and her energy was off the chart. Suzy and Karen were the two who were going to be roommates, and I felt like they were a good match being the two youngest.

Bree really loved Karen, and throughout the months to come, they grew a very special bond, at least Bree felt that way. Karen also arrived with her mother and her sister. They were both so excited for Karen to be there. I did the same as I had Jewel and Suzy, walking them through the paperwork and the house. Karen was a blast, and she just made you feel so loved when you were around her. I think her energy was almost comparable to about four energy drinks or maybe a pot of coffee; it was awesome. Her personality filled the room the moment she walked in.

When Bree showed up with Jezzy, it was very interesting. This woman was so tall and had this almost Viking look to her. She began clinging to Dorothy right away, and I didn't think anything of it at first. Dorothy was loving having everyone in the house. Although I do believe it was a bit overwhelming for Dorothy at first. She was an only child, and she didn't even have sleepovers except for a few times in her life. This lifestyle was completely different from anything Dorothy had every experienced, but she loved it.

Jezzy was there to meet me and had questions about my testimony. She wanted to start stepping out and praying for others, so she came to just see my lifestyle because my friend had shared with her some of my videos that I had made earlier in the year. It was a blessing to have a house full of life and good food. I spent the day with everyone, bouncing from one amazing conversation to another. I was so thankful that the girls were settling in their rooms, and it seemed as though everything was coming together.

On September 5, I turned forty years old, and it was the same day that Bree, Dorothy, Jezzy, and I all headed to San Antonio for the upcoming conference. We ended up stopping at a brother's tattoo shop. I had connected with him during my visit to Texas in early April. It always amazed me how the Lord provided so many connections for me in April when I had no idea that He was going to call me to live in the same area. Father definitely had a plan.

Dorothy decided to bless Bree and I with some fresh ink, which was so sweet of her. It was my birthday present, and Bree just wanted to get a tattoo with me. Hers was beautiful and ended up being flowers with the writing, "Peace will win, and fear will lose." Mine was a henna-looking piece. I had researched henna and saw that in some cultures, it is applied to a bride to adorn herself for her husband on their wedding day. I thought, *Hmm, well, He is my bridegroom, and I am His bride*, so I picked a beautiful piece for my right arm and hand. I still love it to this day, and it was a gift from Dorothy, which made it even more special to me.

Jezzy started saying things to Dorothy that neither of us understood. Like at one point she said, "You are not forgotten, Dorothy." Another thing she kept saying was, "You're not in Zara's shadow, Dorothy." It really started pressing on my heart, and eventually, I asked Dorothy if she felt that way. She assured me that she did not and didn't understand why Jezzy was saying those things. It became really strange the more we spent time with Jezzy.

At the time, I didn't have an understanding of the fact that there were seeds of division being planted. Whether Jezzy knew she was doing it or not, I have no idea. Dorothy and I never had any trouble communicating, and she never wanted to be the one to lead when we prayed for people or really when we did anything, including decision-making. Dorothy constantly would tell me she hated making decisions and would have me lead most of what we did. I had no problem leading, but it was strange the way that Jezzy was speaking to Dorothy almost as if I was leaving her behind because I was leading.

Looking back now, I see so clearly how and what happened. It was literally the enemy planting doubt and insecurities in Dorothy. I truly wish I would have prayed about what was happening at that time, but I didn't think twice about it until the Lord revealed it to me later.

Once the "Cultivate Revival" conference began, we were all settled in and ready for a wonderful event. Robby Dawkins was the first to speak, and his beautiful wife, Angie, was there as well. We were actually able to spend a little time talking with them once the event was over for the day. Angie Dawkins was kind enough to pray blessings over me as well. Bree was excited because even though she had met and taken a picture with Robby in Michigan, this was a bit more of an intimate meeting place. She actually had time to ask questions and spend a moment in conversation with Mr. Dawkins.

Then it was time for Randy Clark. I got a moment to ask Mr. Clark a few questions because I was really trying to understand some things I had been witnessing. When I spoke with him, he shared that he had only been "slain in the spirit" (fell back while being prayed for) a few times in his entire life. I asked him why people would fall down when I prayed for them, but yet I didn't feel a thing. His reply was, "It isn't about what you feel, but what God is doing through you and how they are being touched by the Lord that matters." I mean, what could I say to that? I knew it wasn't about me. I just didn't fully understand what it meant or was all about. So I accepted his answer even though it still didn't give me any understanding. All I could and did take from it was that the Lord does things we don't understand sometimes.

> **Lord, my heart is meek before you. I don't consider myself better than others. I'm content to not pursue matters that are over my head-such as your complex mysteries and wonders-that I'm not yet ready to understand.**

I am humbled and quieted in your presence. Like a contented child who rests on its mother's lap, I'm your resting child and my soul is content in you. (Psalm 131:1–2 TPT)

Then Bill Johnson took the stage. I was ready to hear what he was going to preach. I really was hoping for some kind of answer even though I wasn't sure of the questions I had. All I knew was that my life had shifted, and I was desperate for someone to tell me something. Everything was so different, and I really felt like I knew nothing even though when God provided moments for me to speak, it was as if I knew so much. Weird, right? It sounds crazy and seems even crazier to confess, but I believe the Lord can do anything when we are surrendered and open to Him. I knew and know God is amazing, and that surrendering to the Lord is a huge key to having a relationship with Him. I'm not sure what I was seeking. Maybe just someone to tell me everything was okay and that God had a plan? I don't know, but I wanted to talk to every preacher who was walking in the same things I was because perhaps they could give me insight or a better understanding or a "word from the Lord." It was wrong of me to seek answers from men or women, honestly, but I had a lot of growing and learning to do at this time.

Praise God! He is faithful and walked me through all of this. When Mr. Johnson was done talking, I went up and shared with him just some of what had happened to me throughout the year, and all he said was, "Wow, He really just threw you in, didn't He?" That was it. He blessed me with a book and signed it and said a prayer asking the Lord to bless me, and that encounter with Bill Johnson was over in minutes. The one thing I came to understand after meeting the "big name" preachers was that they are just men and women. They are just like me in the sense that they have the same Holy Spirit as I do. I had to learn that when I need guidance or answers, the best place to turn is to my Bible and in prayer with the Lord. I was just experiencing so much so fast and listening to way too many people rather than just resting in the Lord! It wasn't that the people I met were wrong. The truth is my seeking through people was wrong!

It was really confusing when I started listening to a lot of sermons from different ministers because they would talk about double portion, double anointing, all of these words and things that I wasn't seeing in my Bible or had ever heard of. Many times, they were referencing when Elisha asked for a double portion of Elijah's spirit in the Old Testament. I saw what they were referencing but was challenged because we now have Holy Spirit who is more than enough. I had to walk through some valleys to come to the understanding that there is no need to chase some special anointing because through Jesus Christ, filled with Holy Spirit, is all the anointing we need.'

That took a long time to understand, and the Lord had to really work on my heart because I kept hearing prayers for double portions, more of Holy Spirit, and so many other things that seriously confused me as a new follower; and I had no one to help me understand. Dorothy didn't ask questions like I was and couldn't answer some of mine; she just followed and believed. For me, I needed to know that what I was following was of the Lord. I didn't want to walk blindly into believing something just because the preacher said it was so. I was challenged by the manifestations, how to really handle casting out demons, the shaking I saw people doing, the falling down, all of it.

As we were coming to the closing of day three of the conference, I began feeling like we needed to skip the last day and head home. I couldn't explain why, but I just knew that it was time to head back to the house. Dorothy and Bree both agreed, and Jezzy, well, she wasn't very happy with the decision, but we were her ride, so she really didn't have a choice.

The school was holding a large welcome party for the students on the eight, and although Bree had agreed to go to the conference instead, I felt the Lord was telling me she needed to attend. It was so obvious that we were meant to be at home once we arrived there. Jewel, Karen, and Suzy were so happy we were home and welcomed us with much love. My two other renters had just arrived as well: Lee, who was fifty-five years old, and Agnes, who was the oldest of the house, after Dorothy, of course.

Lee had come in from Michigan and was such a sweet woman. She was super fit and a bit of a health nut, so she was so happy there was a gym available in the garage. Lee was a wonderful addition to the house and was extremely full of joy. She and Dorothy really hit it off and became close right away. Lee was so kind and had handcrafted glasses for every woman in the house with scripture added and all. It was so sweet of her. We were all so happy to be together and were ready for whatever the Lord had prepared for all of us.

The Lord himself goes before you and will be with you; he will never leave you nor forsake you. Do not be afraid; do not be discouraged. (Deuteronomy 31:8 NIV)

Agnes was a health nut as well. She was just a little older than Lee and just as sweet of a person. She had a kind spirit about her and was very childlike. Agnes had come in from California. She had some different ideas on food, like she only purchased the healthy expensive stuff, including her coffee. I respected that but have never been worried about all the statistics or anything like that. She seemed so wise and knew a lot about foods and other things that I had no clue about. So there we were, a house full of eight women who didn't know one another (minus Dorothy, Bree, and myself), ready and willing to serve the Lord in whatever He called us to.

I was so glad we came home early because all the ladies, including Bree, were able to go to the school for their welcome party. I hadn't seen Bree so happy in a long time. She had Karen and the other ladies surrounding her, and I just felt like this was going to be life-changing for her, and it was. All the ladies of the house were able to walk into school together and share in that moment. I was so thankful.

The next day, Jezzy had her flight back home; and although I had love for Jezzy, there was something spiritually off with her that I didn't understand. She also prayed over Dorothy that day, and I listened as she, again, mentioned Dorothy not being in my shadow, which began to truly stir my spirit. At this time in my life, I didn't have any understanding of how to pray against things like that. The ladies and I had planned for our first "family meeting" that evening as well.

Before Bree took Jezzy to the airport, I asked all the ladies if they would like to pray with me for Jezzy, and all of them were more than willing. It was awesome as we all stood around Jezzy to simply bless her and pray for her knee that she had, had damaged for a long time. When Suzy put her hand on Jezzy's knee, it was the most beautiful site because the knee popped and was healed. When Jezzy tested it and shared that it was healed, Suzy was bouncing off the walls. She was so excited because she had never had anyone healed through her prayer, and it sincerely warmed my heart. I couldn't even have imagined what the Lord had in store for all of us in the coming months.

That night, as we all gathered together in the living room, each of us shared our testimonies and how we ended up there at the house, the school, and in Texas. There were tears and laughter throughout the hours we spent together that night. The moments and memories that were built that night are some I will always hold dear.

Every single one of us has a story. We are created to encourage one another and lift one another up, even in the midst of storms. Our testimonies are meant to encourage, and these beautiful ladies were overcomers. When everyone shared their stories, I believe that as we listened to one another, it gave us a better understanding and awareness of one another. I don't think anyone even knew, but this was also the very first time I heard my beautiful daughter share her testimony. I can't express how heartbroken yet overjoyed I was to hear her share her heart. I realized that some of what my daughter had to overcome was me. She had to overcome her mom being a drunk, and she shared how the Lord had truly healed that between us. It was powerful and hard for me to realize that I, too, had played a role in hurting my daughter. I was beyond thankful that God had brought us both to the place we were in that very moment.

The first day of school came, and you could literally feel the excitement in the house. The ladies were up early and ready to roll. I got up the first day in order to take a picture of all the girls. I was just as excited for them. Dorothy and I spent the day in our Bibles and just sharing about how much we loved the ladies and the fact that we could see God had placed us all there. It was so surreal the way everyone was like-minded and in the fact that we all just wanted to grow more in the Lord and follow Jesus.

When the ladies got home it was so much fun to listen to them share about the whole experience and how it was affecting them. I was a little shocked at the way the school was set up. It was literally a huge sanctuary, and everyone was in the same place. There were small groups that met once a week, but it was just like a big conference with different speakers coming in throughout the weeks, sharing their hearts, testimonies, and theologies.

I confess that I didn't expect it to be like that; but honestly, I wasn't attending so I suppose I really didn't know what to expect. I also had never even heard of a ministry school until April when I attended my very first conference. Honestly, I didn't even know anything about conferences either until I saw one for the Power and Love earlier in the year when I was at my mother's. I was so new to the whole thing, but I knew that as each day passed, the ladies would come home excited. They all felt like they were growing and learning more and more, so with that, I was excited for them.

I loved hearing them share their day and all they were learning. I tried to make sure that I was there every day when they got home so that they could share and so that I could support them. Bree came home a few times and just fell into my arms sobbing. I would look at her and ask if she was okay, but she would just smile at me with the most beautiful shine and tell me the Lord was showing her so much.

Next scheduled at the house was a birthday party for Dorothy and Agnes on September 15. I let the ladies know that they were welcome to invite anyone they wanted and that the house was always open for them to have friends over. Some of the girls invited people over for the birthday party and barbecue we were having that Saturday. I, too, invited a few friends who I had connected with as well.

On the morning of the barbecue, I ended up having a brother in Christ call me and ask me if he could bring a woman over to the house with him who he had been praying for. He explained to me that she had demons and needed freedom. I didn't hesitate to say, "Of course, bring her over, bro." I had seen and experienced enough that demons didn't scare me or worry me in any way. I may not have known much, but because I believed in my Bible, I knew I had full authority through Jesus Christ.

The barbecue was so much fun, and there were a lot of people who came to celebrate with us. When my brother in Christ showed up with his friend, everything in the house got real. As soon as the woman he brought walked into the living room, she ended up standing completely still. She didn't even make it all the way into the living room. She stood right by the hallway to my bedroom which was off of the living room. Now the living room, kitchen, and dining room were all connected and only separated by half walls, so it was a very open floor plan.

As I was leaning on the counter, I looked up at the woman to find she was staring at me and growling. Her face began to shift in ways that our faces don't normally shift, and all I said was, "Oh, this is happening." I instantly walked over to the woman and asked her if I could pray for her, and she simply nodded her head yes. I laid my hand on her forehead and began praying. I commanded any unclean spirits to leave her, and as I did, she jerked back. I just continued to pray over her when all of a sudden, her entire body went limp, and she fell to the floor.

I had some friends over that I had just met who were a married couple, and both were ordained ministers. Earlier in the day, they shared with me that they saw me as a jigsaw puzzle and that

God was putting all my pieces together, which I thought was a pretty cool word. The husband walked up to me and told me I needed to ask the woman if she had been baptized when she woke up. I agreed and said, "No problem. Good idea." I didn't think of those things. I was like a new born baby with the Lord. I just blindly believe what His Word says and follow His lead.

There are many moments that I wish I didn't hear half of what I did through the conferences and others I had exposed myself to. Honestly, some of it ended up making me question what I knew the Word said, but again, that was something I had to grow threw, throughout these years.

I swear the woman was out cold on the floor for almost forty minutes. People had to even step over her. I was still adjusting to seeing things like that. When she started moving and shifting, I went over to her and kneeled down. I asked her if she was okay and how she felt, and she said she felt better. I asked her if she had ever been baptized and given her life to Christ, and she said no. So I asked her if she wanted to, and she replied with tears in her eyes, "Yes."

I went straight to my bathroom and began filling up my bathtub. I then went to the ordained minister and asked him if he would be willing to baptize her. I still wasn't comfortable or had much understanding that I had the authority to baptize. I didn't know what to say or how to do it or even if I should. I was thankful when the man said he would. So a bunch of us loaded up in my bathroom, and the very first, of many, was baptized in my bathtub. When she came out of the water, we all prayed over her, and she began to manifest again, but this time she, spit a huge loogie out. It was pretty gross, but I had definitely seen enough deliverance videos to know that demons come out in puke, spit, coughs, and the like. I knew at that moment that the woman was set free.

I realize that for someone who doesn't know or hasn't seen, all of this may seem unbelievable. Please keep in mind that I am not trying to convince you of anything. I am simply sharing what I experienced. Consider it a short testimony. I say short because there was so much more that happened over this entire year that I am not writing here because this book would probably never end.

The night exploded from there. We had one young man who even *pretended* to manifest a demon. When I stopped praying for him because something in my spirit told me to pull back, and a brother also confirmed what I felt as he whispered in my ear that I should stop praying, the guy I had been praying for just started laughing. Then he said, "See, that's why women shouldn't be in ministry." I was so taken back. My heart just hurt for the guy. I told him he should go talk to some of the other guys in the house so he could get some understanding. There was another lady who was healed and another who was set free. It was a complete explosion of heaven on earth. Kingdom as we are called to live. It was the wildest barbecue I had ever had.

For weeks, the ladies and I joked about having a *barbecue*, always referring to deliverances, healings, and kingdom. The house never slowed down from that day forward. We even had a group of three or four students who lived at the "men's house" who pretty much lived at our house. They were brothers in Christ who wanted to spend as much time at our house as they could. I think a lot of days when school let out, the boys would just come to hang out. The only topic we talked about was Jesus and how to walk out what He calls us to.

> **I tell you this timeless truth: The person who follows me in faith, believing in me, will do the same mighty miracles that I do-even greater miracles than these because I go to be with my Father! For I will do whatever you ask me to do when you ask me in my name. And that is how the Son will show what the Father is really like and bring glory to him. Ask me anything in my name, and I will do it for you! (John 14:12-14 TPT)**

As the days went on, the girls grew closer and closer. Bree was so happy to have the sisters she had always wanted, and she was connecting so much at school. Bree, Karen, and Suzy even played in the rain together; it was so good to see Bree so happy. Suzy and Karen were so silly and the perfect fit for each other. Along with the way that Agnes and Lee connected, all was well. Jewel was a bit distant from everyone, but all of us did what we could to keep her involved in conversations and spending time with all of us. Jewel was what I call a "wall walker." She did everything she could to walk along the walls and never be in the middle of a room.

Dorothy and I discussed the fact that we both felt there was something demonic going on with Jewel. I even had a couple of the girls come to me with the same concern. I was praying on how and what to do with that and hadn't felt the Lord lead me to do anything yet. Suzy was seriously the best baker I had ever known. My goodness, that girl could bake some of the best homemade bread I ever tasted. The house had harmony, and there was so much laughter and joy that it was an absolute blessing.

On September 17, we had our first Bible study. There were so many students who started to come over and just hang out at the house; it was unreal. I shared my testimony and would just share whatever the Lord put on my heart. The Lord used me in so many amazing moments of just sharing and pouring into others it was overwhelming. I would sit back so often in the middle of the night alone and just cry, simply thanking the Lord for all He was doing.

Within the first few weeks of school, we had hundreds of people in and out of the house. We held gatherings, Bible studies, movie nights, you name it. There were many times that students would come to me and ask questions. Somehow, I always knew what to say, and if there were times I wasn't sure, I didn't hesitate to say, "I'm not sure. Let's look that up in scripture." It was so surreal the way the house was moving and all that was happening. It was awesome because each week, we had Bible studies, and students, including the ladies of the house, would come to me and share how the speaker that day discussed the same things I said the night before. It was because we follow the same Holy Spirit.

There were a lot of moments when I saw things I had zero understanding of, like the way some students would just start shaking the moment I would begin to pray for them. The Lord had to reveal to me that some of it was Him, and other times, they had grown up in the charismatic, and it was just a natural reaction because they had done it for so long. Talk about wild, I had never even been exposed to anything like it in my life. Now my floor from the living room, kitchen, and dining room literally had bodies lying on it, and I was stepping over people to pray for more, and then they would just drop.

God was doing so much that my mind couldn't even comprehend. I met some students who were so lost, and all the information that was being given to them at the school was just drowning them. Others were doing amazing and taking everything in and growing. At one point, I had a schedule full of meetings for different students each day because I was discipling and helping them make sense of the abundant information being given to them.

I was still connected with some of the leadership at the school as well, and they would reach out to me because they were excited about hearing all that was happening at the house. At one point, one of the staff told me that they had to release one of the other leaders because she was actually putting witchcraft over the students. I had no idea what to do with that information. My daughter was attending that school, and honestly, I did all I knew and began praying. At this time, the students were asked to stop praying over one another, yet they were still encouraged to go on the streets and evangelize. Well, actually, they were required to go out and pray for everyone they could in the community and then report what would happen.

I couldn't even begin to tell you how many students came to me who felt ashamed because they didn't even want to go get a gallon of milk. They felt like they had to pray for every person they saw, and it became works, not heart. It was an evangelist school, but I didn't feel like the pressure to pray for everyone was right. Of course, other students were excelling and doing amazing, so I had no idea how to look at it.

To be very honest, I am still not sure; it is just something I am thankful to have been a part of and am just as thankful that the Lord took me away from. It was hard to see so many loving people struggle just because they didn't understand their identity. All I could do was encourage them to know that sometimes, our life lived is louder than our voices.

Dorothy was loving the house, but there were real challenges growing between us because I barely had any time to give her my attention. I balanced a lot of meetings, and there was always a house full, but she wanted all of my attention and felt left behind. It wasn't the truth. I adored Dorothy. I cooked dinners for her and clipped her toenails. Yup, I went there. I just wanted to honor her, but I also had a calling to help others. It was a very straining time in our friendship.

I can't even begin to tell you how many times in the middle of the night I would just lie prostrate (it means lying flat, submissively. I had to look it up the first time I heard it too, no worries) on the floor literally crying to the Lord. I would ask Him to protect the ladies in my house and to lead me on how to help the students. I would beg Him to show me what my role really was there.

My biggest heart cry was how could I help Jewel. She was still very distant and withdrawn. She was so quiet, and I knew there were issues, but I didn't know what I could do to help her. Suzy's mom came over for a visit as well, and that just about shocked me because of the conversation I heard them have. Suzy was just sitting there trying to share her heart with her mom. All of a sudden, her mom looked at her and said, "Get behind me, you spirit of rebellion." Suzy just rolled her eyes, and it instantly broke my heart. What the heck was going on? Why did everything have to be a spirit of something? I was seeing and hearing this more and more.

There were some really cool moments during our Bible studies. I remember on one of them we had a house full, and all of a sudden, I knew that God was showing me something was off. I walked around the house praying and asking Father, "What is this? What are you showing me?" I found myself standing in the kitchen looking at my living room, and there was like a thick cloud above everyone's head filling the living room. I stood there with this dumbfounded look, asking the Lord to show me what to do.

Lee walked over to me, and she said, "Zara, what are you thinking? I can see on your face something is going on."

I asked her, "Do you see a cloud in the living room?"

She said she didn't, so thinking about how Elijah prayed for Elisha's eyes to open, I reached over to ask the Lord to open Lee's eyes. As soon as I touched her, she started to fall back. I instantly let go of her and realized that wasn't going to work like that. Finally, I heard the Lord say, "Witchcraft is in your house."

Oh, right then, I got really loud and asked for everyone's attention. I explained that we all needed to pray, right now. I led the prayer and simply said something along the lines of "Lord, this is your house. I invite you to flood this house with your presence and make anything that is not of you so uncomfortable it has to leave. In Jesus mighty name." It was incredible. Within five minutes, a particular young lady left the house, and the entire atmosphere shifted back to normal. I had several kids come up and tell me how strange that was and how they knew something was really off because even their conversations were weird. Can I explain how or why? Nope! Do I understand it? I believe I do, and all I can say is God is good.

For the kingdom of God is not a matter of talk but of power. (1 Corinthians 4:20 NIV)

There were many nights that particular students would come over and wait until everyone left so they could talk to me individually. One evening, a young man who was really suffering from depression and other issues ended up staying until 3:30 a.m. We talked about how the Lord wanted Him free and how he needed to be renewing his mind in the Word. It broke my heart to see how he just couldn't comprehend that it isn't complicated. It is literally believing what the Lord says above everything else. I cried for that young man, and even though I knew he had been delivered earlier in the night from some very demonic spirits, he still couldn't embrace how much the Lord loved him.

I believe that we are our own worst enemy and that the battle to believe things we can't see is some of the biggest tricks the enemy uses on us. If we push all else aside and just say, "I trust you, Lord, even when I don't understand, even when I don't see, and even when I don't feel right. I trust you with all that I am," I believe that alone can bring us freedom, but we can't stop there. We have to push on and spend time in the Word. I ask the Lord often to embed His Word deep in my heart. I pray that my roots be so strong in Him that when the storms come, I won't shift. It doesn't mean that I walk this out perfectly, by far actually, but I am able to see clearer and handle things with faith, knowing that I am not facing trials alone.

Dakota was going through a really rough time back in Indiana. His girlfriend had broken up with him, and he was fighting to get his visitation to see his daughter. See, his girlfriend and her family owned an employment office in Indiana and were very wealthy. Let's just say they are extremely connected with people in authority. So after discussing it with Dorothy and both of us praying on it, we allowed Dakota to live in Dorothy's empty house in Indiana, with a few rules, of course. It was to enable him to have a place for visitation, and even though he did, his girlfriend was still only allowing him visits when she wanted or felt like it. Dakota also called and shared that he was waking up in the middle of the night with massive pain in his face, so the girls and I surrounded the phone and prayed over him. I would call and check on him often.

Lee ended up inviting some friends over for a homecooked meal. She was always so kind and thoughtful. It was truly a blessing just to be in that house every single day. We were all growing and sharing with one another in the excitement of living for the Lord. It was church every day as it should be and how it was in the beginning:

> **Daily they met together in the temple courts and in one another's homes to celebrate communion. They shared meals together with joyful hearts and tender humility. They were continually filled with praises to God, enjoy-**

ing the favor of all the people. And the Lord kept adding to their number daily those who were coming to life. (Acts 2:46–47 TPT)

One time, during one of our gatherings, I had this impression to go sit at the dining room table where a bunch of students were eating. When I say house full, I mean that there were usually always over twenty people or more. I think the biggest gathering we had was near to eighty people in the house, if not more, so these weren't small groups (just to give you an idea). Anyway, I had no idea why or what I was supposed to say, but I went ahead, was obedient, and sat at the table. I began simply sharing what was put on my heart, and it was such a God moment because the students' eyes were huge as they stared at me.

One of the students kept looking at me funny, and I kept teasing him because I didn't understand why. I would say, "I see you looking at me funny." Then I would laugh and continue on with what I was sharing. Finally, the young man spoke up and said that he was born deaf in one ear and that as I kept talking, his ear was popping. I got super excited and ended up asking him if I could pray over him. With him in agreement, I walked over and laid my hand on his ear and commanded the ear to open, and the next thing I knew, he fell right over into his buddy's lap who was sitting next to him. The report came in the next day that the young man's ear had opened, and he could hear. Seriously, what do you do other than give God all the praise!

I think it goes without saying that the month was filled with so much joy, peace, and the overflowing presence of the Lord. I spent more time than I could even write about giving God praise and being overwhelmed each and every day. My daughter was happy and growing. Dorothy and I were overcome by all that was happening, and the atmosphere of the house was indescribable. There were countless nights of worship and simply surrendering our hearts to the Lord as we loved Jesus and allowed His love to consume us.

CHAPTER 12

THE DEMONIC

October 2018

It was amazing how badly some of the students wanted a word from the Lord but weren't taking the time to sit and listen to him. The Lord revealed to me that doing this was like the Israelites after Moses led them out of Egypt. The Israelites were afraid the moment God showed up. The people asked Moses to speak to them rather than listen to God themselves.

It isn't okay to always seek answers from others. I have had to learn that I can be fed some really good advice and some really bad advice, but no matter whether good or bad, I need to always take it to Father. There are those moments you know God is speaking a word through another. He will also speak to you if you're just willing to listen. It is a dangerous place to be if you are only wanting to hear through others and not listening to Him yourself. What I am saying is that sometimes we need confirmation from the Lord, which sometimes will come through a brother or sister in Christ. However, don't get caught up chasing a word from the Lord and not taking time with Him yourself. If He if going to speak to you through someone, when they speak, you will know whether or not it is from Him. He has given us discernment; we just need to learn to use it.

> **When the people saw the thunder and lightning and heard the trumpet and saw the mountain in smoke, they trembled with fear. They stayed at a distance and said to Moses, "Speak to us yourself and we will listen. But do not have God speak to us or we will die." (Exodus 20:18–19 NIV)**

Things began to become more challenging for me personally. I felt like it would be wrong to share some of my challenges with the ladies because they were there to grow closer to God. I guess I thought I would be a stumbling block or something. One of the things that were really hard for me was when students would come to the house only because they were hearing about my blessings and how God was moving there. I actually had one kid come up to me and didn't even introduce himself. He just said, "Hey, are you Zara?"

I smiled and, of course, told him I was.

He then said, "Will you pray for me that God will open up finances and bless me as he has you?"

I instantly said, "Well, how about you tell me your name first?"

It was things like this that I didn't have a grasp on until I spent time with the Lord, and He revealed how to handle them. I was in a deep study one day because it was happening continuously, and I was desperate for what to do. People were coming to the house asking for me to pray that what God had done for me He would do for them, and then they would leave, never even acknowledging my existence as a sister in Christ. I suppose it wasn't as bad as the kid who was legally blind, and by the end of the first semester, so many people had prayed for him, yet none of them even knew his name.

We have to remember that this is more than just signs and wonders. Without love, it is all for nothing! We need to see the heart of others and not just chase what God does through us. Our testimonies are meant to encourage others in faith, not to become our ministries or to replace the Gospel.

The Lord had me in a deep study of the ten virgins found in Matthew 25:1–13. At first, my thought was, *Dang, these chicks were selfish for not sharing their oil.* It was so funny because the Lord corrected me quickly as He revealed to me that the oil represented their intimacy, their relationship with Him.

> **At that time the kingdom of heaven will be like ten virgins who took their lamps and went out to meet the bridegroom. Five of them were foolish and five were wise. The foolish ones took their lamps but did not take any oil with them. The wise ones, however, took oil in jars along with their lamps. The bridegroom was a long time in coming, and they all became drowsy and fell asleep. At midnight the cry rang out: "Here's the bridegroom! Come out to meet him!" Then all the virgins woke up and trimmed their lamps. The foolish ones said to the wise, "Give us some of your oil; our lamps are going out." "No," they replied, "there may not be enough for both us and you. Instead, go to those who sell oil and buy some for yourselves." But while they were on their way to buy the oil, the bridegroom arrived. The virgins who were ready went in with him to the wedding banquet. And the door was shut. Later, the others also came. "Lord, Lord," they said, "open the door for us!" But he replied, "Truly I tell you, I don't know you." Therefore keep watch, because you do not know the day or the hour. (Matthew 25:1–13 NIV)**

It almost knocked me off my chair when I heard the Lord say, "Zara, you have been faithful. Even when you took showers with four gallons of water, you were grateful." I was rocked to the core. See, I had struggled most of my life. There was a time when Bree and I lived in Michigan in an old travel trailer for about two years, and we didn't even have hot water. I would warm the water on the stove and then fill four-gallon jugs to be able to take a warm shower, but I didn't complain. Truth is, I was just thankful for the water and the shower. The Lord was revealing to me that my journey was just that, my own.

The relationship and the time I spent seeking Him when no one was looking wasn't something I could just lay my hands on and impart to someone else. That was one of the stretching moments that I had to walk through in order to have a better understanding. There were so many of those kinds of moments for me throughout this time in my life. I still have moments where I am taken back by Father's faithfulness and how He will reveal new things to me. I believe that is the beauty of knowing Him; there is always more to grow in. There is always more understanding to come to. There is just always more with Him. It is a lifetime relationship. He's not something we just try.

As time went on, Bree and Karen grew closer. I was so thankful for their relationship. Bree had even come to me and shared how much she loved having Karen in her life. On the night of October 4, Dorothy and I were sitting in the living room, and the house was pretty still. All the girls were upstairs, and here came Jewel. She warmed up her coffee cup in the microwave, and I felt led to ask her a few questions. As she stood with her back pressed against the wall, she shared that she was struggling pretty badly. She shared that she couldn't even worship at school without feeling like something was strangling her, and she confessed something was wrong with her. I won't give too many details, but she shared a lot. I asked her if it would be okay if Dorothy and I pray for her, and she agreed.

Jewel sat down on one of the stools next to Dorothy's chair, and we began to pray. It was the strangest feeling. As I placed my hand on Jewel's head, all of a sudden as I was praying, I felt like something was almost trying to crawl up my arm. I can't explain it any better than that. It was like a disgusting feeling, and I knew it was not of God. I began using my other hand to swipe it off as I continued to pray. Jewel began manifesting and growling a bit, but it was obvious that this thing wasn't going anywhere. I didn't understand but decided to do the only thing I knew:

> **Again, I give you an eternal truth: If two of you agree to ask God for something in a symphony of prayer, my heavenly Father will do it for you. For wherever two or three come together in honor of my name, I am right there with them! (Matthew 18:19–20 TPT)**

I went directly upstairs and woke everyone up, asking if they would come to pray with Dorothy and I for Jewel. Not one of them hesitated. It only took minutes until every single one of the girls was downstairs, and we were standing around Jewel praying. It was such an intense night, and nothing was leaving, but Jewel was definitely manifesting. Before we knew it, the sun was coming up, and I told the girls I would reach out to one of the leaders at the school. Surely, they would know what to do. This is what they were teaching the students to walk in—not just casting demons out, but identity, authority, and kingdom. So I reached out and was told to bring Jewel in to meet with one of the leaders named Mickey.

With zero sleep and my heart hurting for Jewel, we loaded in my truck and the others girls in their cars, and we all headed to the school. When I walked in, I felt so welcomed because I had already met so many of the students at the house and had visited the school a couple of times previously. Plus I saw a few of the leaders of the school who I just loved.

Jewel and I found Mickey while the other girls headed to the sanctuary for class. As we walked, I explained to Mickey most of what happened throughout the night and explained that I didn't understand what to do. Mickey looked right at me and said, "Don't worry. You and I are on the same level. It's no problem."

I felt relief yet also thought to myself, *Wait, I don't believe I am on your level because I have never seen anything like this*. This was also my first encounter meeting Mickey. When we sat down, Mickey began talking with Jewel, and we ended up praying for her. I have no idea what happened other than there was some kind of a shift. Mickey looked at me and asked, "Did you feel that?"

I nodded my head yes even though I had no idea what I felt, but it was definitely something. That was pretty much it. Mickey said Jewel would be fine and asked if I would like to join the class with her for the day, and I said yes. So off Jewel and I went to head to the sanctuary for the day. It was an hour or more of worship, and then a speaker came out and spoke for a few hours, and then we were headed home.

I reached out to Jewel's mom that day as well. I truly wanted to honor her and keep her posted because once we were able to talk alone, Jewel expressed to me that nothing was different. I was so lost on why or how this was even happening. I mean, I had several experiences at this point with deliverances, but the demons always left. This thing wasn't going anywhere, and it left me puzzled because all I could think was that we have full authority through Christ, so why isn't it leaving?

It was during this week also that Jewel asked me if I would baptize her. Oh, my goodness, what an honor and blessing that was. I agreed, and the house gathered together for Jewel's baptism. She was the first person I ever personally baptized. A few minutes later, Karen also made the decision for Jesus and asked me to baptize her. It was beautiful, and we all gathered to celebrate Karen's baptism as well. I truly believed that things would change for Jewel after she got baptized, but it seemed to make things worse.

This is when I began down a rabbit hole of researching deliverances. I was reading every book I could get my hands on and watching videos on YouTube in hopes I could have some better understanding. I read every scripture that had anything to do with demons or casting them out. The main thing I saw was Jesus was short about it. He was pretty much, "Shut up and get out," not verbatim, mind you. I was spending every minute I was awake praying and seeking answers to why Jewel wasn't free. I even asked the house if they wanted to join me on a four-day fast; some did, and some didn't.

On October 10, I arranged another meeting with Mickey because Jewel was sharing with me how something was physically hurting her and she was uncomfortable. This time, when we got to the school Mickey, Jewel, and I went into a private room. Mickey prayed over Jewel and it was extremely short, then he looked at her and told her to go to class. When we were alone, Mickey explained to me that he had spoken with some of the other leaders and they believed Jewel had been assigned there as a distraction. I cannot express how those words pierced right through me. What? A distraction? They wouldn't even have known anything about Jewel had I not brought her and shared what was happening. Mickey asked me to bring Jewel back the next morning to meet with another leader, that was above him.

On October 11, there we were, Jewel and I, Mickey, and this higher leader in the school. They expressed to Jewel that perhaps the school wasn't a good fit for her and that they were a school, not a church. She was told, right in front of me, that they believed once she was out of there, perhaps she could find somewhere to find freedom. My heart was crushed and not to mention super confused. The entire thing threw me into the humblest place I had ever been. My heart cried for Jewel, and I wasn't about to just walk away from her. Mickey ended up sharing with me, privately, that he felt that Jewel was a distraction to my calling, and if I needed help getting her out of my house, the school was willing to help with that. I told him that I appreciated the offer, but I could handle the situation. To be honest, I was praying so much, and all I could hear Father say was, "Zara, I've called you to lay your life down for others, and that looks like something." I believed that meant I wasn't supposed to send Jewel back home worse than when she had arrived.

Greater love has no one than this: to lay down one's life for one's friends. (John 15:13 NIV)

October 12, while I was downstairs in my kitchen, I began to hear noises upstairs. It was like, *thump, thump, thump, BANG!* It was so loud. I looked at the ceiling and thought, *What the heck is that?* and there it was again. *Thump, thump, thump, BANG!* The kitchen was right beneath Jewel's room, so I knew where the noise was coming from, but I had no idea what it was. So I decided to go upstairs and find out.

I have never physically felt anything like this before or since, but when I walked up the stairs and to Jewel's bedroom door, it was like I walked into a literal wall of fear that hit every single part of my body. I literally turned around and said, "Nope." When I got downstairs, I sat down trying to figure out what happened and prayed over why I felt the way I did. I thought, *Why in the world did I turn around?*

The very next night, the same thing happened. *Thump, thump, thump, BANG!* This time, I wasn't going to allow anything to stop me. I marched up the stairs, and there was that wall of fear again. It was so physical and so real, but I walked right into it and knocked on Jewel's door. When she opened her door, I swear to you, it was like looking something so evil straight in the face, and it was not Jewel. Her hair was down, her body was different, her voice was different, and all I could see was pitch-black in her eyes. And behind her, in the room, all of her lights were off. I said, "Hey, honey, I just wanted to see if you were okay."

She said that she was, so I told her I wanted her to come downstairs and talk to me. I was shaken a bit, but I was not going to allow whatever this was to cause me fear.

When Jewel came down, I asked her what was going on. She began to explain to me that she was slamming her body into her furniture. She said that when she was alone, it was worse than it had ever been, and *it* was telling her to hurt herself. Jewel confessed that she wanted freedom, but that the voice was so loud, and she was losing hope. There were so many things she shared with me that night, including having suicidal thoughts and more. I cannot express how many tears I shed for Jewel when I was alone with the Lord. Here was a beautiful young woman who wanted freedom. Why was she not free? As I held her, I told her I would not give up and that I would walk this out with her. In prayer, I knew Father was telling me to stay by her, but in my mind, I was lost as to what that looked like.

After speaking with her mother and receiving full authority from her to do whatever I felt the Lord led, I took Jewel's door off the hinges of her room. Jewel had given me full authority as well because she said she wanted help. I felt that it would be safer for Jewel if she didn't have the privacy to act on whatever voice was talking to her. I spoke to every woman in the house, and we all agreed to fight for Jewel no matter what it looked like.

So it began. The girls and I had worship music playing upstairs at all times, and Jewel was not left alone. Except for when she showered, went potty, or went to bed, of course. I reached out to Mickey and asked him to please not kick Jewel out of the school and to give me a little time to see if I could help her. He agreed and told me to keep him posted.

I began looking up deliverance centers near us and found a church that one of the students had suggested. It held deliverance meetings every Sunday. On October 14, I canceled Bible studies for two weeks with students and asked everyone to stand in pray for our home, which seemed to bum some kids out, but that was okay. I had no idea what I was doing, but I knew that God was a good Father. In that, I had no doubt and had a lot of faith. Several of the girls and I ended up going to the church that Sunday, and it was definitely different. The worship was almost like a hard rock, which I'm not against, but it's just not my cup of tea. Then after the service, they invited anyone who needed deliverance into this small room. It was the kids' room in the church because there were toys, and the walls were painted for kids.

There we were with Jewel, supporting and loving her. The preacher's assistant put trash cans at the end of each row of chairs, and the preacher began to share that if anyone felt like puking, coughing, burping, or spitting, they could grab a trash can because demons can come out in different ways. He said he was going to begin reading down the list and commanding any demons to leave.

I thought the whole thing was very strange, but there we were. He literally had a piece of paper with a list and began praying and commanding demons to leave.

I realize it wasn't a funny situation because as he read down the list, there were a couple of people who actually were experiencing deliverance. However, at some point, Bree let out this loud belch, and all of us turned to look at her. It was absolutely normal for my daughter to burp as loud as she could, but I truly don't believe she was thinking about the situation and where we really were. When we looked at her, her eyes got huge, and she said, "It was just a burp, I swear. It was just a burp."

Our entire group began laughing and tried so hard to do it quietly. It was something Bree has been teased about since. The pastor even put his hand on Bree's shoulder at one point and asked her if she was okay. She just looked so embarrassed and said, "It was just a burp." Jewel found no peace there, and the preacher ended up talking to us and taking Jewel and I into a private room.

I'll be honest. I was shocked as he shared with me that he has seen demons that won't leave and that Jewel needed an exorcism, not a deliverance. I was clueless about all of this and didn't even know there was a difference between the two. I don't believe that there is a difference after walking through all I have, but I am also not claiming to have a ton of wisdom on this.

We ended up scheduling a time for the next day for the preacher to come to the house while the girls would be at school. I asked Dorothy that evening to please go with the girls (anyone could pay for day sessions at the school if they weren't a student) because I didn't want to expose her to some crazy exorcism. The preacher had told me that he had witnessed things being thrown, shelves being knocked over, and more during "the process." I just felt that it would be best if Dorothy wasn't at the house because I honestly had no idea what to expect. He also sent home some papers for Jewel to fill out.

That evening, she and I, on occasion with her mother on the phone as well, filled out this crazy paperwork. It was literally asking about her parents, her grandparents, and their parents. It asked about anyone in her family being involved in the Freemasons or watching *Harry Potter*. I mean this questionnaire was wild. I had never seen anything like it.

On October 15, this specific preacher came to the house with his assistant, and all the girls, including Dorothy, had gone to school. Jewel and I were the only ones there, so the preacher had all four of us sit in chairs, and then he faced Jewel. To this day, I am not sure what I witnessed, but all I can do is share with you what happened. The preacher took his Bible and began quoting:

> **Though one may be overpowered, two can defend themselves. A cord of three strands in not quickly broken. (Ecclesiastes 4:12 NIV)**

He began circling above her head with his Bible as if he was binding her with a cord while he was saying this scripture. Then with his Bible still in his hand, he stated something like, "I take my Bible, this Word of God, and use it as my sword." At which time, he placed his Bible on Jewel's stomach, and she literally reacted as if she was stabbed in the stomach, sunk down in the chair, with her arms to her sides tightly as if they were actually bound, but there was nothing there visible.

The thing that happened next was what completely shook me. I was watching Jewel's face the entire time, and when he put that Bible on her stomach, there were literally black lines appearing under her eyes, and she changed. She looked just like she did the night I went to her room when I heard the noises and she opened the door. She began laughing with this deep dark voice, and I assure you, she was a soft-spoken young woman.

He then proceeded to command the demon out and to leave. Jewel or whatever *it* was just laughed at him. It was like some freaky movie. I sat silently as I watched and listened. I had no clue what to do with what I was witnessing. As time went on, there were some things said in the Darth Vader–sounding voice coming out of Jewel, and then the preacher would rebuke it. I can't even tell you how long this went on.

In the end, the preacher said he would need to come back, but I was done. This was enough. I remembered a very close friend in Indiana who spoke highly of a deliverance center in Arizona months prior. She had driven all the way there to seek freedom and received it. After the preacher left, and Jewel was normal again, I shared with her about the place and asked if she wanted to go there. She was open to anything. We discussed what had happened, and I told her that this was the last thing I knew to do. I called her mom and explained what happened. I told her that the place in Arizona is all I know to do, and if that didn't go well, there was nothing more I could do. Her mom was so thankful and said she understood.

I reached out to my friend and got all the information on the center. She was still highly recommending the place. I then got ahold of the deliverance center, set up an appointment, and made all the arrangements for Jewel and I to fly out on October 17 with her mom flying to Arizona on the eighteenth. She wanted to meet us there.

I continued to have the full support of her mother and Jewel. I had no idea how long to book the trip. I mean, I had never even seen or been a part of anything like this situation and had no clue what I was even doing. So I ended up booking the trip for ten days. Dorothy agreed this was a good idea, and she fully supported it. She was upset when I asked her to stay home and take care of the girls and the house. She was not happy with me because she wanted to go everywhere I did, but after all I had been witnessing, I just knew this wasn't something for Dorothy to be a part of. I also called Mickey, and although he shared that the school didn't believe in such places, he still told me to keep him posted. All he explained when I asked him what he meant was that they believed that when you tell a demon to leave, it should leave or you move on. At that time, I was simply not in agreement with that because I knew the Lord called me to walk this out with Jewel.

All the girls were told about the trip and most of what had happened that day. I tried to keep everyone posted in the house as to what was going on, but there were some things that I didn't feel the Lord wanted me to share. I stayed open to suggestions because I really didn't know what else to do. On October 17, Jewel and I were on a plane headed to Arizona. Dorothy was still a little upset because she wasn't going, but she ended up leaving me the most loving note in my Bible, encouraging me that she was praying and supporting me.

When we landed in Phoenix, we picked up the rental car and headed over to our hotel. There was some kind of church service that night that the woman from the deliverance center suggested we go to. While sitting there listening to the person preach, I just didn't fully agree with some of the things being said. I kept an open mind for the center though because this was just a small church and only a suggestion that we went ahead and followed.

That night as we were getting ready for bed, Jewel kept saying things like, "It (referring to the demon) doesn't like that we are here. It doesn't like you, Zara."

I just laughed and responded with, "I really don't care what it likes. I really don't like it either." She shared with me how she was feeling and how it messed her up inside. I just tried to show her love and encouraged her that God is good and everything would be okay. It was crazy as I laid down to sleep, I had the most vivid vision of Jewel on top of me stabbing me. I knew it was just fear trying to take its root in me, so I giggled and thanked the Lord that He is my defender. I slept like a baby.

The next morning, Jewel's mom came into town, and we ended up going to the deliverance center. It was almost like the other preacher as far as all the paperwork and history questions about her and her family. Jewel's momma was there now though, so she was able to answer a lot of the questions and dive deeper with the woman working there.

Jewel's mom shared with me about how she had known there was a presence with her daughter, but that she was really hoping that by attending the school, she would find freedom. I told her that I really thought the school may be kicking her out and that after this trip, I didn't know if there was anything else I could do to help. I loved them both very much and made sure to tell them that. They both expressed how much they loved me as well and appreciated all I was doing to help.

On the first night, after all of the questions, the woman took us into a little sanctuary that had the lights off. She began praying with another woman over Jewel. It was super different, and I'm not sure how I felt or, even to this day, feel about some of the things that were said. They began commanding Canaanites, Amorites, Hivites, and I think almost every *-ites* found in the Old Testament off of Jewel. It was absolutely bonkers to me. I didn't have judgment. I just don't and didn't have understanding at all. I can't say I do or ever will in my lifetime.

When they were done, the woman set another time with us to come back the next day. I was not sure about any of it and told Jewel, once we were alone, that if she didn't want to go back, it was okay. Jewel did share that she had felt something leave and felt some relief, so she did want to go back for one more day. I agreed to take her back. It was the first time that she had shared that she felt better. Jewel's mom was only able to stay for a couple of days, but I was so thankful that she made the trip.

I don't know what I was expecting, but I know it was definitely not what I was hearing or seeing. The woman at the deliverance center was very friendly and shared a lot of testimonies with me, which I appreciated. I'm sure they see deliverances, but I didn't understand the way they were getting there. I am not dismissing their center, but I don't see Jesus doing or saying any of what they were, and He is who I follow. They even teach that movies like *The Shack* and others are "open doors" for demons.

Personally, I enjoyed the movie *The Shack* and couldn't imagine it opening doors for the demonic, but again, that is my opinion. It is literally a beautiful depiction of Father, Son, and Holy Spirit, but I'm sure others would disagree. Well, this center definitely did. I actually do believe that there are certain things we can expose ourselves to that allow the enemy to have a place in our thoughts and minds, in our lives, but that would be a whole other book.

Jewel and I attended one more session, and I spent time continuing to talk with the woman at the center. Some of her testimonies were seriously mind-boggling, but I know God can do anything. This ended up giving Jewel and I eight more days in Arizona before our flight home. During that time, we mainly watched *School of Kingdom Living* with Dan Mohler. There was also a worship concert with Andy Mineo, KB, and several other artists that I was supposed to go to with Bree. I was a little bummed, but circumstances didn't allow me to be there, and that was okay. So I live streamed the event so that I could sort of be with Bree while she was there. Now, my security cameras at the house were connected to my phone, and one day, they kept going off. When I checked them, I laughed so hard.

See, I hide the thermostat that was located upstairs so that none of the ladies could mess with it. While I was gone, Dorothy ended up telling them where it was. So my camera would ding, and there would be Lee coming out of her room, lifting the picture the thermostat was under, and adjusting the temp. Then five minutes later, here came Agnes out of her room, adjusting the thermostat again. Three minutes later, here came Suzy. Well, you get the picture. I ended up messaging all the ladies in our group chat and told them, "Stop messing with the thermostat. If you are cold, please put a sweater on. If you are warm, get a fan." Lee ended up messaging me and telling me that Dorothy seriously seemed lost without me there. In a lot of ways, Dorothy was reliant on me. In some ways, it wasn't healthy and was really hard for me to cater to her needs because I had so much on my plate. I truly tried to honor her in every way I could though, but some things were out of my hands and in His.

I usually spoke with Dakota over the phone about once a week or so, and he knew all that I was walking through. I believe the Lord gave him such love and a heart for Jewel even though he never did meet her. He would tell me he was praying for her and that he didn't understand why, but he loved her and was worried for her. I thought it was so sweet that the Lord had planted a real love for Jewel in Dakota's heart.

Dorothy and I also stayed in close connection. I was calling or texting her daily and always keeping her posted on what was happening. There were some crazy moments during this trip with Jewel. On day five, I was encouraging her to stand and worship with me. When she stood up and tried to lift her arms to the Lord, her neck had impressions on it as if hands were actually strangling her. I saw it with my own eyes. She had already shared that she was held back from worshipping, but seeing it was an entirely different thing for me. At one point, she began manifesting really extreme growling and face shifting—all of it. I just simply wrapped my arms around her and sang worship songs while I rocked her for over an hour. It was absolutely confusing to me why she wasn't experiencing freedom, and I continued to pray, asking and begging God to reveal the truth to me.

On day seven of our ten-day trip, the truth came out. I was walking around the hotel, praying, when the Lord said, "She is lying. The spirit is a friend to her, and she finds comfort with it." I was livid instantly. I couldn't even wrap my head around it. I had witnessed so much of this demon-twisting Jewel up and making her hurt herself, and all the while she was actually embracing it. It was also revealed to me that she had been hurting herself far longer than she had shared with me. Oh, I was not happy at all—after everything, after all that we had shared and walked through. Yeah, livid is putting it lightly. I ended up praying more about what Father wanted me to do, and I heard, "Just love her." I took a little time to breath because I knew that if I just walked into the room, I would go off. She was lost, and going off on her wasn't going to help anything.

When I walked into the room, she was sitting on her bed, and I stood at the end of it. My first words were, "You have been lying to me this entire time." I did get a little loud as I tried to speak through my tears. By this time, I was hurting so much for her. She was believing a lie and found comfort in this demon because she had built a relationship with it. I could see all of it so clearly. When she was younger, she was diagnosed with scoliosis and was unable to move around for years. She built hate toward everyone around her, and that was the entry point of the demon. She enjoyed fantasizing about some really demonic things, and in the end, the demon provided her with this twisted comfort of not being alone.

Over the last few days in Arizona, we talked and walked through a lot of things. I just loved her as I knew I was called to. She truly gained freedom from so much wrong thinking, and if I hadn't listened to the Lord, I don't know what would have come of it. Jewel confirmed everything the Lord had revealed to me and even apologized to me. She expressed how much she loved me and continued to thank me for not just giving up on her. I ended up making arrangements with her mom, and she was coming to help Jewel pack and take her home. It was all set and scheduled for the day we were to arrive back in Texas.

I spoke with Mickey, not going into full detail with him, but he expressed to me that they were not going to allow her back at the school. He explained that when she returned to Texas, she could come up and grab a check for half of her tuition that she had already paid. It was bittersweet to know she was leaving, but it was time, and all that needed to be done was done.

On October 27, Jewel and I were standing in line to get on our plane when my phone began to ring. I had our tickets in hand, was making sure Jewel was good, and not to mention my luggage. I reached around and saw that it was Agnes, but I knew I would be home in a few hours and could share what was happening with all the ladies together. At least, that was my thought process as I dismissed the call. Plus I was beyond ready to be home and get settled back to normal if you would call our lives *normal*. I didn't think anything of it again as we loaded the plane and headed home. It was so good to walk in the door and feel the comfort of being home. I can't express how thankful I was. I wouldn't say I was drained, but I did miss my daughter and Dorothy tremendously.

Dorothy told me that Agnes had packed a suitcase and gone to a hotel for the night, which confused me a bit, but she was a grown woman. I shared with the girls that Jewel was going to be heading home, and soon after we arrived at the house, Jewel's mother showed up.

Jewel did meet with Mickey at the school, and half of her tuition was returned, which I thought was awesome that they did that for her. Jewel did share with me that Mickey told her that he was not in agreement with me taking her to Arizona and that he thought I was wrong for going to a deliverance center. I thought, *Well, that was nice of him to share. But, oh, well, my path was not his, and it was something I had to walk through.*

When Jewel was all packed and they were ready to leave, there were a lot of hugs and love showered on Jewel and her momma. Her mother ended up taking me to the side and handed me a $1,800 check. She said, "I believe in the ministry God has called you to, and I can't thank you enough for all you have done to help my daughter." My heart was so touched, and it was a blessing I didn't see coming at all. Ironically, throughout each semester, I had students who would come to me and bless me with money. They would just share that the Lord put it on their hearts to tithe into the house.

Once Jewel and her mom were gone, Agnes ended up coming home and asked to speak with me. I went up to her room and closed the door behind me. She shared with me that she felt that I shouldn't be helping younger girls if I can't even answer my phone because they need to know I'll be there. I was honestly speechless. She went on to ask questions that all I could say was, "I'm really not sure, sis." It was like I was expected to have an understanding of what I had just walked through when I had none. Agnes also shared that she had to leave the house because I didn't answer the phone to talk to her. She continued to say that she loved Jewel, but she was in a place with the Lord that she just couldn't allow anyone to disrupt. I sincerely had no idea how to respond to her, but I did my best to show her love and support. I did feel that everything she said sounded extremely selfish and with zero compassion.

When I was done talking to her, I left her room and went into Jewel's room to pray over it. Jewel and her mom also left the entire brand-new bedroom suite that they had delivered to the house, which, I knew, would bless the next student who would move in.

I discovered that my olive oil bottle was upstairs, and I realized that the oil had been put on EVERYTHING! Doorknobs, windows, I mean everything. I think half a bottle was used. That made me a little upset, and I ended up asking the girls to please never do that again. I explained that the oil was symbolic, but it was the power of Jesus and His name that anointed the house. I believe they were just operating out of fear more than faith. It honestly felt like there was no care or consideration about the fact that I had been gone for ten days with Jewel. They didn't know what had happened in full, but they didn't even consider the challenges, nor did they even seem to try. I wasn't and didn't look for attention, but I surely didn't expect to come home to what I did.

Would I like to say that it would have been nice if someone would have educated me or helped me gain an understanding of deliverances? Sure, but the truth is that I needed to walk through this experience in order for the Lord to teach me, to grow me, and to prepare me for the future. Did I see it during this time? Oh, no, I definitely did not, but I do now. I can't even begin to tell you how many deliverances I have walked others through since this experience. The power and goodness of God are indescribable.

I had been praying for understanding, so He put me in a situation that helped me gain understanding. In the end, many people told me to just walk away from this dear sister, but God used this to grow me. Several people, including Mickey, ended up speaking against my decisions behind my back, but it was okay. That was and is between their hearts and Father.

Speak blessing, not cursing, over those who reject and persecute you. (Romans 12:14 TPT)

Just because you may not have an understanding of something someone else is walking through doesn't mean God's hand isn't all over the situation. If you start to believe that you understand the plan God has for someone else's life, well, you may be in a dangerous place. Yes, perhaps He will give you a word or a vision for another person, but do not assume you have the full view of

His plan for that person. There is growing, and there are things they may have to walk through that you will not understand. We spend so much wasted time judging people while sugarcoating it with Jesus. When the fact is, we are actually in judgment when we think things have to be the way we have experienced them—as if God fits in our experiences alone. He does not, I assure you. Ironic how assuming can be and usually is judgment.

This was the time in my life when by walking through what I did with Jewel, I grew so much in the understanding of deliverance and how we can give demons permission to stay with us. I learned that when we hold onto unforgiveness, bitterness, or anything that is not of God, it actually gives the demonic authority and the right to stay. It doesn't matter how many people lay hands on you, if you're comfortable with your demons and don't truly want freedom, they aren't going anywhere.

I cannot express how thankful I am for the time I had with Jewel. Even though it was some of the craziest experiences I had walked through up to that point in my life, I was thankful. I saw Jewel and her mom again in the Spring of 2019 when Dorothy, Bree, and I, plus some of the girls living with us, went to Georgia on our way to "The Send" conference in Florida. She really looked amazing and was doing so much better. In the end, Jewel messaged me a few times throughout the years. She even sent me a picture with her and Pastor Dan Mohler. My prayers are with her and her family always.

It wasn't long, and the house was back to the flow of things. Bible studies were rescheduled and in full swing. The house was full of students again. I also began to purchase everything for a huge Thanksgiving dinner. I posted on the school's site and invited anyone who wasn't going to be able to make it back home. I planned to make the biggest dinner I had ever cooked. I even purchased two countertop roaster ovens. I just wanted to bless students who were stuck in Texas, so they didn't have to celebrate Thanksgiving alone. Before I knew it, Halloween came, and Bree put on her CatDog onesie to pass out little keychains that said, "Jesus." We had a few students join us to pass out the keychains, and the girls had a fun night telling all of the kids who came to the door that Jesus loved them.

I know, I know, it happens every year and probably happening to some of you right now as you read this. GASP! NOT HALLOWEEN! I will close with this revelation the Lord gave me a few years back. Every year, there are so many posts from believers as they talk about the devil and how dark Halloween is, how it is the most demonic night of the year, and how there are satanic rituals and sacrifices unto the enemy—all that stuff. I am sure there is. I have no doubt. However, if darkness isn't the issue and the absence of light is, isn't it ironic that in order to not celebrate or participate in Halloween, we just have to shut off our light? Just let that sink in. Do with it what you want. I, however, believe that if by chance, the only time a kid comes to my door is Halloween, then I have an opportunity to shine the light of Jesus because He lives inside of me. I will let my light so shine. I will give out a Jesus keychain or cool cross keychain and say, "Hey, Jesus loves you." You do with the holiday what you want.

CHAPTER 13

THE FAITH

November 2018

The start of the month was amazing. The ladies of the house didn't seem affected much by all that had happened with Jewel, but I believe they were pretty focused on their schooling and growing. I was still struggling to understand, but I didn't share everything with anyone, except the Lord. I was confused why some of the things had happened the way they did. As for any relationship with Mickey, well, he became very cold toward me any time I saw him after this. That lasted the entire time I was in Texas and was involved with students. However, I took those emotions to worship and prayer.

I don't believe anyone knew how much I was struggling after walking through everything I did with Jewel. I would just spend most of my days in the Word, and once the girls were home, we would have a house full of not just the girls but other students as well. I also began discipling and meeting with students who I had been meeting with before my trip to Arizona. They were so patient in waiting for me to get back but expressed how much they missed talking to me. I soon began to just feel freedom as I released any and all confusion to the Lord.

On the morning of November 9, I was at home studying the Word when my phone began to ring. On the other end was my brother's best friend, Jack. He said that Dakota had collapsed in the house and was laying on the floor unconscious. Jack told me that the ambulance was en route to get Dakota, so I told Jack that I would be on my way there as soon as possible. After hanging up, I told Dorothy what happened, and we both agreed that I needed to go right away.

Within twenty minutes, I had my plane ticket printed and my rental car locked down for when I arrived. I was packed and headed out the door. I received another call on my way to the airport. It was one of Dakota's other friends who was already at the hospital with him. She said that Dakota was conscious enough to tell her to call me. The hospital wanted to send Dakota to a bigger hospital because they were small, and he needed more tests and diagnoses that they couldn't provide. So she asked me which hospital I should have them take Dakota to. She gave me two choices, and I picked St. Vincent Hospital, in Indianapolis.

Once I was on the plane, I sat down and realized that I was not afraid. There was no worry or freaking out. I actually had peace and knew God had Dakota in His hands. I was almost shocked at how my emotions were so calm, and I thanked the Lord. I knew the peace I was feeling was supernatural, but I also knew that Dakota's story wasn't over. I stood firm in believing that!

A gentleman sat down next to me, and once everyone was on board, the plane began to take off. As I read my Bible, the stewardess came around passing out drinks, and the gentleman next to me ordered a Jack Daniel's and coke. I knew he had been drinking already; there was no denying the smell of alcohol on him when he sat down next to me. As the flight continued, we started to talk, and he shared that he was a missionary kid. He said that his parents traveled on mission trips his whole life, which I thought was really cool. As he continued to share his story with me, he made the comment that he and God had an agreement. He said that he knew he shouldn't drink, but that God knew his heart, and it was okay.

Funny how I didn't say a word about him drinking, yet he felt the need to justify himself. I explained that I didn't judge him, and it wasn't my job to tell him that he was wrong for drinking. I began to share how alcohol had such a grip on me at one point in my life and how I didn't sleep. I shared how I thought that the only way I could sleep was to drink. I told him that there were times when I didn't want to drink but still did anyway. I explained how God saved me and the moment I met Holy Spirit and how he burned addiction out of me in an instant. I shared my entire testimony of what the Lord had done in my life since January and how I wasn't the same person anymore. He was touched by my story and began to ask questions. I told him how much Jesus truly does love him and that we all have a choice. I don't believe God is in heaven looking down, disappointed, and in complete shock at the decisions we make.

Actually, I truly believe God loves us just the way we are so much that He doesn't want to leave us there. That means that as we wholeheartedly pursue Him through relationship, He will completely transform our thinking. He will even change the way we react to situations. When we surrender to Him, there is a shift, even in our emotions and how we handle what we say.

I didn't try not to cuss; that would have been weird. He just changed the way I talked. It doesn't mean God can't handle an *f*-bomb, so don't hear that. What I am saying is that where the Lord had taken me at this point in my life wouldn't have been as affective if I was standing in front of others using swear words. It was definitely not their tribal language. However, if I'm speaking to a bunch of bikers or at a bar, my language isn't the same as it may be in a church speaking to a bunch of ladies. We seriously need to stop twisting the Lord's Words to fit our opinions. He is God; we are not.

Now I am not claiming that I never say a cuss word, but I definitely have a Holy Spirit filter and respect others when it comes to my language. Some tribal language includes what others wouldn't, and it's not considered fowl. I enjoy the show *History of Swear Words* on Netflix, with Nicolas Cage. It is actually informative. I completely have zero judgment if you disagree; that is okay. I just encourage you to pray and talk to Father about everything. Always follow His lead! To better explain, our tongue is a two-edge sword. We can encourage and lift someone with our words or we can chop them up and tear them down with our words. I have sisters that if they see me, they call me their 'bitch,' but the intention and meaning is completely endearing and loving. I have other sisters that find the word completely offensive and I would never say it in front of them. We should not claim that what we may find offensive, while others may find it endearing, is fowl. If the heart of the person is in no way speaking fowl or ill things, perhaps we should stand back and ask Father to take our offense away. There are different tribal languages all over the world. Look up how the Irish speak in Ireland. Some of their words, as Americans, we would find offensive. Could the bigger problem be picking up offense just because others do not speak the same as we might?

Do not let unwholesome talk come out of your mouths, but only what is helpful for building others up according to their needs, that it may benefit those who listen. (Ephesians 4:29 NIV)

As the time went on, for the two-and-a-half-hour flight, we shared and talked about the Lord the entire way. Once we landed and were allowed to exit the plane, I honestly walked as fast as I possibly could to get down to the car rental in order to rush to the hospital. As I was almost running, I heard someone yell for me, and I stopped to turn around to see the same man I was sitting next to during my flight. He was running to catch up with me. He stopped in front of me and said, "Hey, I know you are in a hurry, but I was wondering if you could pray for me." In that instant, I realized what a divine appointment this entire moment was and asked him to sit down with me. We ended up sitting down in some of the chairs at an empty gate in the airport. We talked a little more, and I asked him what he would like me to pray for. Through tears, he confessed that he was an alcoholic and some other things I won't share here. So I placed my hand on his shoulder and began to pray over his situation and asked the Lord to bring him peace. It was such a precious moment.

When I was done praying, the gentleman walked with me through the airport until it was time to depart ways. I gave him a great big hug and told him Jesus loved him very much and then headed down the stairs to the car rental area. When I arrived to pick up my rental, the clerk told me that because I didn't have the physical driver's license and only my paper license, they couldn't rent the car to me. See, it was only a few days prior that I had finally had the opportunity to trade in my license to obtain my Texas driver's license. I felt this overwhelming panic and anger try to take hold, but I took a deep breath and asked for the manager. It took forty-five minutes of talking and making a phone call to Texas to finally confirm my license was valid. After all was said and done, the manager handed me the keys to my rental. I was a little concerned about my brother being in the hospital by himself because his friend couldn't go with him to Indianapolis. I just didn't want him to be alone.

Once I was able to get loaded into the car and begin my trip, I realized I was another thirty minutes from the hospital. I went as fast as I could without breaking the law, and when I pulled into the hospital parking lot, I jumped out and ran into the building. I found where my brother was, and when I walked into the room, the nurse actually explained that he had only arrived just ten minutes ago. God amazes me every day. His timing is so perfect. If I had not taken time with the man at the airport, if the car hadn't been delayed, I would have been at the hospital way before my brother had even arrived. However, God knew and set everything up so that I would walk into that hospital room at the right moment.

Within your heart you can make plans for your future, but the Lord chooses the steps you take to get there. (Proverbs 16:9 TPT)

At that point, no tests had been run, and the nurse was preparing to take blood and begin the process. Dakota was in and out and not fully aware of what was happening, but he knew I was there. He would wake up and tell me that he loved me and talk for a few, not making much sense, but then fall back out of consciousness. At one point, I asked him if he would like me to call our mother, but he said no and told me he would prefer that I didn't. The night was long, and the nurse kept trying to get me to go to the family waiting room, claiming I should sleep, but I refused to leave Dakota's side.

I read my Bible to him the entire night. There was another time the nurse came in that night and asked him if anything were to happen, would he want them to resuscitate him, and he looked at me and shrugged his shoulder. I told him absolutely, but he did mention to her that he didn't want to be on a ventilator. I, however, intervened and explained that they were to do what they needed to take care of him. He wasn't even making sense, let alone able to make conscious decisions like that.

On the morning of November 10, a team of five doctors came in and said they were still waiting for some results to come back from the tests they were running. Now there was an hour that family members couldn't be back in the ICU area, and I was required to leave, so I decided to go to a nearby restaurant to grab a bite to eat. The moment I stepped outside, I realized I was in Indiana, and it was November. I was freezing, and I even had flip-flops on. I hadn't considered the weather at all when I left Texas. So first, I ran to the nearest store and grabbed some warmer clothes and then hit a restaurant.

As my food arrived, my phone rang, and it was the lead from the team of doctors who were treating Dakota. She explained that if they didn't put him in an induced coma and on a ventilator with a trach right then, he would not make it through the day. She asked me what I wanted them to do, and I explained to her that I wanted them to do whatever it took to help him. After I hung up the phone, I began praying about what I should do. Should I call our mother, or should I not? I knew Dakota asked me not to, but at this point, things were too serious not to. I felt the Lord led me to go ahead and make the call.

When my mother answered her phone, I explained what had happened and that I was at the hospital with Dakota. I told her that I would call as soon as I knew more. When I got back to Dakota's room, the doctors came in and explained that Dakota had a blood sugar of 1,691. Yes, he should have been dead. He also had pancreatitis, a fungus in his blood, and was in kidney and liver failure. They also stated that Dakota was a diabetic, which was something he had never been diagnosed with before. The doctor said that he was the sickest person in the entire hospital and had a 50 percent chance of survival.

I explained to the doctor to please do everything they could do, and I would do what I knew I could. I looked right at the main doctor and said, "I believe God is going to heal him completely." The doctor looked at me real funny, but there was nothing changing my mind. I continued to have complete peace and felt extremely confident that God would handle all of it. After being told what was going on, I called our mother, and she wanted me to ask if the ventilator was "helping or just prolonging" his life. I took that pretty hard and was upset she would even ask a question like that. I wasn't about to ask that question and didn't.

I then began praying over the specific issues that were wrong with my brother. Even as they began running dialysis, I continued to have complete peace and wasn't bothered. I was not even stressed about what was happening. I had this supernatural peace that I simply can only explain as being from the Lord. I sat by Dakota's bedside the entire time and read my Bible while he lay there in a coma. I had no doubt in my body that he was going to pull through with a full recovery.

At one moment, it was literally only about three seconds. I believe the covering of peace the Lord had blessed me with was lifted, and I felt this caving feeling of defeat. I can't explain it; it was almost like a blanket was lifted off of me, and overwhelming fear came to me. It was only for about three seconds, and I began to speak out loud, "Absolutely not, God, I know you have me and have Dakota. I know everything is going to be okay!" I stood up and began commanding healing in his body again. The feeling literally only lasted for a few seconds and never returned.

I was continually speaking life and healing all over my brother as he laid there with a ventilator breathing for him. Later in the day, I spoke with my mother again and offered to pay for her to fly down. Her reply was that she didn't want to fly and stated she didn't have gas money to drive. So I told her I would give her money to cover her gas if she wanted to come down. I made a couple of phone calls that day. I spoke with Bree and booked a flight for her to also fly up and be there. She was scheduled to arrive the next evening. Another call was to my brother's ex-girlfriend, who had their daughter. She had just taken him to court for child support and had tried to put him on supervised visitation. The decision ended in my brother's favor and him being allowed in his daughters' life without supervision. I knew he had court-ordered visitation coming, and he was obviously not going to make it. I wanted to make sure he was covered, and she didn't try to say he abandoned the visitation.

His ex-girlfriend freaked out on the phone and began speaking death over the situation. She was saying things as if he were already dead. I completely refused to accept that and told her that he would be okay and continued to speak life about and over my brother. With her being an unbeliever, I could hear her speaking from fear and refused to allow her to move me. I knew with all my heart that my brother would be just fine, and I wasn't worried about death. I had zero fear.

The Lord tells us that He didn't give us a Spirit of fear but one of power, love, and sound mind. The enemy is who comes to kill, steal, and destroy. I was not accepting that this was going to be a battle won by the enemy. I refused to embrace even the thought, and I wasn't going to sit there and listen to anyone else speak anything different.

On Sunday, November 11, Dakota's ex-girlfriend showed up at the hospital. I did allow her to come into the ICU to see him, but I refused to leave her alone with him. I wasn't going to allow her to speak anything opposite of life over him. I had been praying and reading scripture constantly and was on zero sleep. She kept making comments to me, saying, "I told him he needed to get his health right," and several other things she claimed. When she stood next to him and said, "I hope this makes you get your life together for our daughter now." I had finally had enough. I stepped up behind her and told her she needed to leave. I couldn't take her there after she claimed that he wasn't there for his daughter. I knew that she had denied him visits for months. I asked the hospital to make her leave, and she was actually kicked off of the hospital property. Oddly enough, the real trial began when my mother arrived soon after this happened. I hadn't spoken with her in months and hadn't seen her since the Power and Love conference back in June.

My mother ended up coming in and trying to take over as if she was in charge of everything. She did end up asking the doctor if the ventilator was helping Dakota or just prolonging his life. It may have been the lack of sleep, but I thought that being her first question was honestly the most thoughtless question a mother could ask in our situation. She was very dismissive of me and extremely rude. I knew Dakota didn't want me to call her, but this was more serious than he realized when he made that decision. For not speaking or seeing one another in so long, this was not the best way for us to come together.

She had even blocked me on Facebook months prior because she couldn't stand seeing my posts about what God was doing in my life. I was marked as Dakota's medical power of attorney, but my mother took over and claimed that since he was unable to sign the paper work before they put him in the coma, she was now taking over that position and making the decisions. The nurses and I spoke because I was so concerned about the entire situation. The nurse explained that if our mother tried to make any decisions against the best interest of Dakota, they would step in. She reassured me not to worry and that nothing would change in their care for Dakota or with any decisions without my knowledge.

Bree arrived in the evening, and she ended up encouraging me to get some sleep. She wanted to sit with Dakota and was going to continue reading scripture to him while I rested. My mother also came to rest in the family waiting room, and it turned horrific, quickly. She ended up telling me that Dakota had told her he never wanted to have a trach when he saw Oliver get one. Oliver was my mother's husband who had passed away years previously, and Dakota was like twelve years old when Oliver got a trach. I looked at my mom and said, "That was then. He is a father now, and things are different."

My mother rolled her eyes at me and began to tell me that I had found God and left her behind. I knew it wasn't true and was getting a little irritated that she would even say something like that. She said several things that were so off that at one point, I actually thought I could make her hear me.

It was as if I could literally feel the arrows of her hate and judgment against me. Mind you, I hadn't slept, going on three days at this point. I ended up pulling a chair in front of her and sat down. In a calm voice, I said, "Listen, none of that is true." I began to explain what had really happened earlier in the year, and she picked up her phone to ignore me. I confess that at that moment, I allowed my anger to take over and grabbed her phone and threw it. She then stood up, and I grabbed her hips and, in my frustration, pushed her back down in the chair and said, "You are going to listen to me."

Then she said, "Who do you think you are?"

At that point, she couldn't hear anything I said. The truth is that she hadn't been able to hear me for a long time. So the fact I had pushed her down just shut her off even more. Later, as I was in tears, I went to the chapel in the hospital and asked God to forgive me for laying hands on her. I remember just begging for His love to overflow the situation. I did end up going to my mom and asking her to forgive me for pushing her down in the chair.

The next couple of days with my mother were ridiculous. She tried telling me that she was a youth pastor, which I knew wasn't true. She tried to tell me about how she was now a prophet whom God gave prophecies to and many other things. She just kept twisting scripture in so many ways, and when I would show her what the Word really said, she would get upset at me. One time, she said that prophecy was more important than the gift of tongues, which is also not true. She referenced 1 Corinthians 14:2–3, but she must have failed to read the rest of the chapter because that is not what Paul says in 1 Corinthians.

It seemed like every day was becoming more challenging with her there. At one point, my mother explained that she had only brought three days of clothes and needed to go back to Michigan to do laundry and get reorganized to come back. I was so ready for her to leave, so that was a relief. Bree stayed with us until the fourteenth and then headed back to Texas for school. My mother left the same day, aiming to come back on Sunday the eighteenth.

Over the next several days, I stayed by Dakota's side. I didn't want him to wake up and no one to be there if there was a chance of that. At a certain point, the lead doctor came in and told me that if Dakota makes it, he had a long road. The doctor said that he wouldn't be out of there until after the first of the year, and he was looking at six to eight weeks of rehabilitation. I just continued to pray and read to him every moment. Before my mother left, I shared with her about a church that was holding a small gathering with some oil that they were claiming was leaking from a Bible supernaturally. The church was only like twenty minutes from her house, and I asked her to please go and grab some of the oil.

I knew and know that the power is in Jesus name, in the blood He shed, and the strips His body took. However, I also knew that scripture talks about anointing with oil. I just figured, *Why not from a Bible that may be leaking it supernaturally?* She was reluctant, but I begged her, and she agreed that before she headed back on the eighteenth, she would go get some. I'm not sure what she thought about it because she had never heard of it, but I was thankful she said yes. I called Dorothy a lot during this time as well. She was such a rock for me and would pray for the situations that I was facing with Dakota and the challenges with my mom.

On the eighteenth, my friend who I had connected with when I went to see Pastor Dan Mohler, back in February, saw my posts on Facebook asking for prayers. She ended up reaching out to me. She actually lived near Indianapolis and asked if she could come up and pray with me for my brother. I was so thankful, and it was such a blessing to see her again. She was one of the women who recognized my voice from my testimony videos, and she had stayed in touch with me. My mother ended up showing up with the oil and said, "I have found my home church."

At first, I thought, *Wait, aren't you a youth pastor at another church?* I believe the Lord stopped me because I knew that it was a lie when she said it, so why say anything? There was no point, and hey, if she found a church she felt at home in, I was happy for her.

> **Beloved, don't be obsessed with taking revenge, but leave that to God's righteous justice. For the Scriptures say: "Vengeance is mine, and I will repay," says the Lord. And: If your enemy is hungry, buy him lunch! Win him over with kindness. For your surprising generosity will awaken his conscience, and God will reward you with favor. (Romans 12:20 TPT)**

That evening, Dakota ended up biting his tongue and something with the bite guard caused him to cut his tongue pretty bad. I just put some oil on his tongue and began praying for him. I took a picture of what it looked like, and the very next day, his tongue was almost healed. I continued to anoint his body and pray over him constantly. I knew the Lord had him, and the only challenge I was facing was just trying to love my mother through this time.

One day, when we left the room for the nurses to clean Dakota, my mother and I sat eating lunch in the hospital cafeteria. She kept trying to use scripture to justify herself and the wrong things she was saying. I am not claiming that I am all knowledgeable about scripture, but I spend a lot of time in His Word. I spend a lot of time talking to Him and being alone with Him. Things she was saying were hitting my heart so heavily, and they were so off that I couldn't just sit there. Then it would happen; she would ask me a question about it.

I would reply and try to explain what the scripture meant, or I would calmly try to help her better understand what she was talking about. Yet that just made her madder at me, and she would get almost hateful. At one point, she said something, and I asked if she could show me where the Bible said what she was referencing. When she took me to the scripture, I continued reading the rest of the chapter, which clarified the one verse she misunderstood. She got so frustrated with me that she said, "I don't know why I can't seem to find or read this right when I am around you."

It got really bad as she continued, and it was as if she felt like we were in some competition of who knew more or was closer to God. It was uncomfortable and straight from hell. I confess, at one point, I said to her, "I don't like being around you, and I am here for Dakota." She replied by letting me know she didn't like me either, and we just ended that conversation with an agreement that we were there for Dakota and that we were going to keep focused on him and his recovery. For some reason, she decided to tell me that she was also taking me out of her will because I was set and didn't need her help. I just didn't respond.

She talked to everyone who would listen in the hospital, and most of the time the things she said were just blatant lies. One particular woman, my mother had been speaking with in the waiting room, ended up coming over to where my mother and I were sitting, waiting till we were allowed back into Dakota's room. It was so strange as my mom confessed to the woman that she was jealous of me when the Lord started blessing me. How she felt like I didn't deserve the blessings and how she had worked all her life. She said it wasn't right that I was handed everything, and she wasn't. I was floored when she said that it was like I stole her life because she was supposed to write a book, but I did instead. She continued to share how she didn't speak in tongues although she had told me back in June she did. It just made me hurt for her so much more, but I couldn't believe the things coming out of her mouth. My jaw about dropped as she continued sharing everything with this complete stranger. The woman just sat there quietly and listened to everything my mother said.

Now the lady was a believer, and when my mom was done, she spoke blessings over my mom and encouraged her to seek Father in the situation. She explained to her that I was where the Lord wanted me to be and asked my mom if she understood that. To my surprise, my mom said, "Oh, yes, I do now, but I didn't at first."

Then the woman looked at me and said, "You pray for your mother a lot, don't you?"

I replied, "All the time."

The woman said, "The Lord says to stop worrying then. He hears your prayers, and He's got her."

The comfort that overwhelmed me at that exact moment was amazing, and I couldn't deny that He was using this woman to bring me peace. My mother didn't react well, but she sat there as the woman shared with me. That sister spoke life into me and spoke so many kind words. She ended up asking me about my testimony, so I shared about all the things Jesus had been doing in my life. She was so encouraged by my testimony. At some point during my time at the hospital, she asked me to pray over her family member who was a patient there. It was such a blessing and honor to meet her and her family.

Even though there were constant challenges, there were some real God-sent blessings as well. I ended up getting all of Dakota's work papers in order, so he wouldn't lose his job. The floods of prayers and encouragement from everyone and everywhere were beyond imaginable. I was so thankful for the people God had placed in my life. A friend ended up starting a GoFundMe for Dakota. It was to help with any medical expenses and Christmas for his daughter, and honestly, he was almost $2,000 behind in child support as well. It was not good, and I wasn't sure what else to do.

My brother in Christ, Dennis, the one from Canada who was healed at the Power and Love in April, ended up messaging me. He said that in prayer, the Lord told him to donate $2,000 to Dakota and it ended up covering all that he had fallen behind in child support. I was just speechless at the miracles the Lord was doing. Even in the valley, He is good. Jewel even reached out to me, and she had been praying and slipped a prayer note with Dakota's name on it in this special prayer wall. She ended up sending me a picture of it, and it was so thoughtful. I was also blessed with the opportunity to talk to and share with the nurses. I prayed for several of them, and it was amazing how the Lord touched them.

Day thirteen of Dakota's coma was Thanksgiving, November 22. Bree agreed to help and cook her first Thanksgiving meal so that any students who had made plans to come over still had that option. I was so proud of her for stepping up and for the fact that her heart was so in. She was nervous, but I had the security cameras and was able to check in on her while she was in the kitchen. We were on the phone on and off the entire day. She was so excited to put the meal together, and I had already purchased all that she needed to make it happen. One of the girls even helped with cooking the ham while Bree cooked the turkey and most everything else. It was a great turn out. I think over fifteen students showed up, and they all broke bread and ate together. There were many compliments on Bree's food, and she was so happy that she actually did it. I believe it helped confirm for her that she can do anything she puts her mind to.

On November 24, fifteen days in a coma and sixteen days in the hospital, the doctors began to lessen his medications, and my brother started waking up. At first, he was freaked out and tried ripping his ventilator out, but I grabbed his hands and kept trying to calm him down. I can't even imagine what he was thinking or how he was feeling at that moment. My brother was pretty strong, so I ended up asking the nurses for help, and they had to bind his hands down so he didn't hurt himself. I kept talking to him and just reassuring him that everything was going to be okay.

As tears rolled down his face, I told him how loved he was and how good it was to see him awake. For some reason, his left eye was literally sideways. So his left eye was not looking forward; it was looking all the way to the left while his other eye was looking forward. It looked crazy, but I didn't care; there he was—awake.

When he shares this testimony with others now, he says the first thing I said to him when he came out of his coma was, "Bro,

I have been in this hospital for sixteen days, and I haven't killed our mother." It's true. I did say that. But it was funny, and I knew it made him giggle inside.

It wasn't long after he woke up that the ventilator was taken off of him. He couldn't speak for a while, but he sure did try. His body was super weak, and he was pretty confused at first. He was responding and squeezing my hand when I would ask him if he was hearing me, and he began to quickly respond with one squeeze for yes or two squeezes for no on questions the nurse asked. My heart was so filled with happiness at that point. He was awake! HALLELUJAH!

The next day, on the twenty-fifth, Dakota was responding and able to talk, not without a little struggle, but he was good. The first thing he did was tell them he wanted me in charge of his medical, and the nurse instantly brought the paper in for him to sign. It should have been done the day he arrived, but we had no idea what was going to happen or that our mother was going to come in like she did. Here he was, shaking, as he signed the paper, sitting up even. Oh, it was so good to see him back. They began to order what they called a "swallow test" so that he could get the feeding tube out. He past everything with flying colors.

On the twenty-sixth, I wanted a bed. I was oversleeping in chairs pushed together and even sitting up sometimes. So as soon as I knew Dakota was good, I booked a hotel room for a couple of nights. I offered the room to my mother as we had been switching shifts sitting with Dakota, but she refused, and that was her choice.

It's funny how when we ask God for patience, He places us in challenges that require us to build patience. He is so faithful and really does answer our prayers—just not usually the way we think it should look. I truly slept like a baby after I got a real shower and laid down. At this point, I had spent seventeen days cleaning myself, brushing my teeth, and all of that out of a sink in the hospital. I was so thankful for that bed, and it felt like I had been given a small piece of heaven that night.

On the twenty-seventh, Dakota was sitting in a chair, eating, and joking with me. He was doing so well. The doctors were shocked at how quickly he was moving, gaining his strength, and eating, and they couldn't explain it. He had no fungus in his blood, had new kidneys and new liver, had no pancreatitis, and was doing better than the doctors could understand. I loved seeing their faces when I said, "It's all Jesus."

I talked to him about needing to get back to Texas, but that I was going to get my truck and be back up in a week. I had a huge Christmas party scheduled on the fourth for all the students who had been at the house because the last day of school was scheduled for December 14. He said he loved me, that he would be okay, and that he would see me in a week. Dakota swore to me that when I came back, he was going to be getting out of there. I just smiled and told him to just get some rest. The doctors continued to reassure me that Dakota was going to need many weeks of rehabilitation, so I didn't really think twice about it. I set up a schedule with my mother so Dakota wouldn't be there alone at any time, and on the morning of the twenty-eighth, I was on a flight back home.

It was so good to walk in the door. I didn't realize how much I truly missed Bree, Dorothy, and all the girls. I couldn't even begin to express how good it felt to sit in my chair, rest in my own bed, and be able to get in my fridge and eat what I wanted. It felt so good to be home and listen to what all the girls had to share with me about school and just their hearts. Everyone had been standing in prayer with me the whole time I was gone. It was something I will forever be grateful for.

On November 30, while all the ladies were asleep, I broke out all the Christmas decorations and turned the house into a winter wonderland. My heart was to bless them all with the house when they woke up, and it worked. I think they were all shocked how everything changed into what looked like a Norman Rockwell Christmas. It was a long month, and I admit, I was so thankful my brother was okay, and I was home.

CHAPTER 14

THE HEART

December 2018

It was awesome to hear the excitement from all the ladies in my house as well. God was moving in their hearts, and they were enjoying school so much. It was fun listening to them share their testimonies and just hearing their laughter again. Bree was growing so much, and I couldn't have been more thankful to spend time with Dorothy again. It felt like I had been gone forever. I was calling Dakota every single day, and he kept telling me that he was getting released when I got there on the fifth. He said he would break out if he had to, but I wouldn't have let him do that. I shared with the ladies how the doctors were shocked at how quickly Dakota was healing and how they couldn't really explain his recovery. They rejoiced with me and seemed so happy.

 I also told them that when Dakota was released, he was going to need to come and stay at the house until his strength came back. I explained that I was going to build the garage into a bedroom for him and that the rule of "no guys upstairs" would still be enforced. To be honest, we had guys at the house all the time. It wasn't like it was something new. I had even sat up until morning hours with some of the guys from the school on occasions, so I didn't think anything of it. I also shared that I wasn't sure when he would be coming but that I would be heading back there on the fifth.

There were only twelve days of school left, well, actually only ten if we don't count the weekends. Dakota only had Dorothy, Bree, and I. We were his family, and we wanted to help him until he was back on his feet. He couldn't even lift a trash bag out of the trash can without shaking at this time. Plus he wasn't willing to go with our mom; our house was the only place for him and the safest for his recovery.

I was in complete shock because all the ladies of the house seemed to have a problem with Dakota coming there. I was told that it wasn't right because it was a "women-only" house. Seriously? Then, Agnes had a really big issue with it because, I guess, her husband didn't like the fact there would be a guy there. I'm being real. They were women who run the streets and pray for strangers, and now helping my brother they had supposedly been praying for by allowing him to have a safe place to heal in the garage was a problem? The man had been in the hospital for almost a month. I was just heartbroken because of their responses. They really expected me not to help him. I wasn't going to turn my little brother away. I explained that he didn't have anywhere else to go and that we were his only family. I shared the fact that he didn't have a criminal record or anything, so I didn't understand. Then it got really weird and turned into complete division and gossip.

On December 3, I got a call in the evening, and it was Suzy's mom. When I answered the phone, she began sharing with me and said, "Zara, the truth is, sometimes we think we are supposed to help people even family, but we're not. Even Karen had a dream about this."

As soon as she said that, I was like, "Wait, what dream?"

She explained that she couldn't tell me, but that Suzy had shared a dream that Karen had shared with Suzy, and it wasn't good. Yup, all that with these Jesus-loving women. I literally walked upstairs and asked Karen if we could talk. I don't go around things or through others, so I asked her directly. Her response was that she "wasn't released to tell me about the dream" and then proceeded to tell me that Suzy shouldn't have shared it with her mom. Yeah, that sounded like some heavenly divine message from the

Lord. I don't and didn't think so. Now it was gossip, and that is never from the Lord.

I cannot express how quickly all this turned twisted. When I spoke with Agnes again later, she said her husband was okay, and she would finish out the semester at the house and then asked me if I knew what Karen's dream was about. I was so flabbergasted. Is this really happening right now? I responded with, "No, do you know what the dream was?"

Agnes looked at me and said exactly this, "Karen said she can't tell me until she is out of this house."

I thought, *This house? The one she was blessed in, loved in, honored in, prayed for in, baptized in? Till she's out of this house?*

I even spoke to Karen's mom who explained that Karen had issues with men, and when I approached Karen about that, she got upset and said that it had nothing to do with her past.

Bree was crushed because from that point on, she felt like Karen hated her because that was how Karen acted. Karen turned into one of the meanest girls I have ever met. She began to isolate herself away from Dorothy, Bree, and I. She got to where she wouldn't even look at me. She cut Bree off and stopped talking to her pretty much altogether, including at school. She and the other ladies came into some crazy agreement on how demonic or wrong it was that I was going to help my little brother. All of them were fine, but now the three of us, Dorothy, Bree, and I, were not.

Somehow, they allowed a lie and some dream, claiming it was from God, to be truth. Yet the entire thing caused division and just a huge negative shift in the house. As if allowing my little brother to live in the garage when he was released from the hospital was the end of all peace in the home. I had a few students come to me and tell me about how the ladies were gossiping to others about the situation at school. Truth is, I don't care what the devil has to say about me. I just encouraged the students to pray for them.

My home was completely divided from that moment on. It was insane, and to be honest, I was thankful that I knew who I was in Christ. I couldn't believe how sweet Karen appeared and pretended to be for months, but after that, she was truly cruel toward my family and I. She acted as if we didn't exist and like there was never love there at all. The way she cut off all love, care, and emotion toward me, my daughter, and Dorothy was seriously demonic. It was uncomfortable to be in my own home. So I finally got sick of it, and I told every one of them to get their shit and get out. If they were going to treat me and my family like that, they could kiss my ever-widening ass!

Okay, okay, that's not what I did at all. Actually, I prayed a lot for all of them. I cried for them while in prayer—A LOT! I bought a special gift and left a kind letter telling Karen I loved her and left it outside her bedroom door. I continued to speak life and love over every one of them because love conquers all. I didn't have a problem with my heart; they had a problem with the posture of theirs. Sorry, I was intentionally being dramatic because, in the past, I would have said way worse. Many of us would have reacted with anger. It doesn't mean the thoughts didn't come or the emotions weren't there. It doesn't even mean that a part of me didn't want to say that, especially after all I had been through, but I trust my Father to handle everything, and I believe His Word.

> **You have heard that it was said, "Love your neighbor and hate your enemy." But I tell you, love your enemies and pray for those who persecute you, that you may be children of your Father in heaven. He causes his sun to rise on the evil and the good, and sends rain on the righteous and the unrighteous. If you love those who love you, what reward will you get? Are not even the tax collectors doing that? And if you greet only your own people, what are you doing more than others? Do not even pagans do that? Be perfect, therefore, as your heavenly Father is perfect. (Matthew 5:43–48 NIV)**

I ended up throwing the Christmas party for everyone on December 4, and I had a house full. There was this strange distance between the ladies and I, but I didn't let it hurt or stop me from loving them. I didn't care what they had to say just because they didn't understand. Dorothy and I blessed all of the girls with gifts, and we had many students who we also blessed with presents. It was an amazing party with worship, food, love, prayers, and so much conversation.

There are times I miss those big gatherings. It amazed me how a lot of the people I met would pray for strangers, tell them how loved they are, and even give their last dollar. We believe God goes after His one; some of us even know we are that one. We will step out for strangers and act as though we are doing good or perhaps we are doing it to prove to ourselves we are good. Yet if you're a believer and fall back or don't do what others think you should, you're instantly "backslidden" and/or rejected by the same people who promote *Jesus* and *love*.

> **So we can say with great confidence: I know the Lord is for me and I will never be afraid of what people may do to me. (Hebrews 13:6 TPT)**

I experienced some real, fake love throughout my years in Texas. What it did was grow me. I came to realize that my love for others is not based on their love for me. I had to go through some tough things and a lot of tears to get there. If my love was based on others' love for me, I would end up crushed, with my feelings hurt, and lost all the time! Jesus is the only one who can complete me, and even when others judge me or hate me, He loves me.

It really takes a lot of pressure off being able to love freely and truly because you don't expect anything back. You just love the way Jesus loves you. Freely you receive, so freely you give. At least that is the way I choose to live. I feel like many of us have this mindset of, "You take care of your family. I'll take care of mine." Could we be missing the fact He says to love even your enemies? Love looks like something, and it's not your comfort level or opinion. It's unconditional without contingencies. Real love doesn't just love when things are good and make sense; real love just simply loves!

My plan was to stay a week with Dakota in the hospital when I drove up, but he was determined he was leaving. His daily reports were mind-blowing and getting better every single day. I began realizing he was very possibly getting released when I went up. So I worked really hard and got the entire garage set up and ready. I made sure Dakota had everything he would need, including his own trash can because now he had to learn to give himself a shot of insulin every day. He was diagnosed with type 2 diabetes in the hospital.

A couple of the young men I loved dearly, from the school, helped and blessed me by building a curtain wall so that there was some privacy for Dakota. I kept the door that connected the garage to the house open at all times. Plus the ladies' shelves and fridge were located there. I just made it so there was privacy for not only Dakota but also for the ladies when they needed anything. I also set up the treadmill so when Dakota had the strength, he would be able to walk on it.

The ladies hadn't been utilizing the gym for over a month, so it was no big deal. I arrived at St. Vincent Hospital in Indianapolis on the morning of December 6. Dakota was seriously being released that day. The doctors had no idea what or how he was able to be where he was in his recovery, but we serve a mighty God who is amazing. I didn't need an explanation because I had one. JESUS IS ALIVE AND STILL KING!

On December 6, my brother refused a wheelchair because it was important to him to physically walk out of that hospital after he was told he wouldn't be able to. He walked arm in arm with me straight out of there. I had to help him in the truck, and he was pretty much worn out after that walk, but he did it. I was so proud of him and so thankful to our Lord and Savior.

Now Dakota's left eye was still sideways, and it really bothered him so much. When we stopped for dinner and to get our room for the night, he was in tears as he shared with me how it was affecting him. He kept telling me, "Sis, it looks awful. I look like a freak."

Once we got to our room and he was sitting on his bed, I said, "Dakota, look at all of what God has done for you. I believe he can fix your eye too." I walked over and laid my hand on his eye and prayed for the Lord to heal his eye and for it to straighten out, in Jesus name. The next morning when we woke up, it was done. His eye was normal, and he cried like a baby. It was beautiful.

I explained to Dakota about the ladies having some concerns and being uncomfortable, but he said he would honor the house rules, not that he could have climbed stairs if he wanted to. The ladies only had five days left of school at this time, eight counting the weekend. Dakota was determined. Once I shared with him about Karen being the worst freaked out about him coming, he was going to win her over.

When we got back to Fort Worth, it was late on the evening of December 7. I drove Dakota past the house and pointed it out as we headed to the Walmart down the street. I realized Dakota had nothing. He had no clothes, he had no toothbrush, he had nothing. When I picked him up, I just brought him a sweat outfit, socks, and a pair of tennis shoes. He needed a little more than that. As soon as I pulled into the parking lot, I told him I would drop him off at the front. I always parked my truck away from all the cars. I don't even think I got it all out, and a woman pulled right in front of me, and I had no way of stopping or turning. I nailed the entire side of her car. She was driving across the parking lot instead of following the lanes. I couldn't believe it; we were seriously so close to home too. It had been a long day driving, and then this.

Long story short, it was her fault; her insurance eventually covered the damages to my truck, and I got Dakota's clothes and food. I had to have the truck towed home because the front bumper was pressed into my tire, but we made it—finally! I showed Dakota around the downstairs and introduced him to Lee and Agnes, and they were very sweet toward him. I showed him his room, and he loved it.

When Suzy and Karen got home, it was so unreal how cold Karen was. To this day, it still blows my mind when I think about her attitude. Suzy went right up to Dakota and gave him a hug and said hello while Dakota just went in for a hug with Karen as he said hello to her. She was so cold and didn't hide the fact she was not happy he was there. It was tough being in that house over the next week until school was out.

It was only days later that Karen and Suzy got approved for an apartment. It was hilarious how friendly Karen became again. She was even joking and laughing with Dakota. I just had no words. Dorothy and I blessed the girls with some housewarming gifts for their apartment, and once they moved out, they never came back to the house. Karen even unfriended me on her social media and never spoke to me again. She also acted as if Bree was a plague, and it did break Bree's heart for a while. I've never spoken with any of the ladies from the first semester since they all moved out. When I did see some of them in the school, during some of my visits in other semesters, they acted as if they never knew me.

Once school was over and everyone moved out, the house was just filled with our family. Dorothy, Bree, and I, along with Dakota, had an amazing Christmas. We spent the entire time laughing, worshiping, and enjoying one another. It was so much fun to just spend the holidays with everyone. I had missed being home, but it was a blessing with Dakota there to be with us as well. I was so thankful and just relaxed for the rest of the year. The new semester was scheduled to begin in January, and I already had renters for three of the four rooms set to move in after the first of the year. There was one room open, and it was so God who had a plan because it was definitely not in my hands. Even Dakota decided to attend the next semester as well.

One day, my brother came to me and said, "Sis, you got to see this." He ended up clicking a YouTube link our mother had sent him, and there she was, with a microphone in hand, in the same church I had sent her to grab the oil. Our mother was standing on the stage giving the testimony of Dakota's healing. She claimed that Dakota had bit his tongue in half and God healed him, which was not true. She said that when she went there to pick up the oil, her daughter didn't know and couldn't believe what was happening and had told her, "It must be Holy Spirit." I am her daughter; I did send her there, and I never said that. There were so many lies. I was so taken back and hurt for her. She was standing in front of a church giving false testimony. That is so dangerous.

> **There are six things the Lord hates-no seven things he detests: haughty eyes, a lying tongue, hands that kill the innocent, a heart that plots evil, feet that race to do wrong, a false witness who pours out lies, a person who sows discord in a family. (Proverbs 6:16–19 NLT)**

Then she ended her testimony with, "I've always raised my kids to know that this is how we fight our battles. We praise." I couldn't help but laugh at that part. WHAT? Did my mom just try to steal my life verse? I'm just kidding. It was so crazy though, and my brother still, to this day, teases me and says, "Well, you know, sis, it is how mom raised us to fight our battles." He's such a butthead.

After Christmas, I was talking with Dorothy and said, "I'm kind of glad we don't have little ones running around here." I am not playing when I say it was less than five minutes later when a young family called me. I loved this family and had watched their beautiful daughter once throughout the semester, but they said there was a mistake with their Airbnb and needed a place to stay for a week. I didn't hesitate to invite them to come to stay.

My family made fun of me so much; it was really funny, honestly. So we had a younger married couple and their beautiful one-year-old move in. The family ended up renting my last room with all the other girls approving of the husband being upstairs, of course. To this day, I am beyond thankful for all God has done, is doing, and is going to do in my life. I'm thankful for the fires, the stretching, and all the people He has brought in and out of my life as well.

CHAPTER 15

THE NOW

So, that is it! That was the year of 2018 for me, from the start to finish. The year that changed my life and the life of my daughter, my dear sister Dorothy, and my little brother forever. I stayed in Texas for three more school semesters. I was there for two years in total. I continued renting my rooms out to students and holding Bible studies every week. The school grew from that first semester just like I did. They made more rules addressing dating and other things they had learned from the first semester. They have changed a lot in their leadership as well and are still continuing to help others discover their identity in Christ. I also learned that I needed to have more rules as far as little things like making renters clean their fridge area once a week.

    I learned that a lot of students came because of a bit of idolization of Todd White and his guest speakers. I addressed that in many of my Bible studies. Todd White grew his relationship with the Lord by spending time alone with the Lord and walking things out. I don't know this from knowing him personally, but I have heard many of his testimonies. I remember when it was shared that Pastor Dan Mohler, who was Todd White's pastor, ended up paying Mr. White weekly as if he were working a regular job so that Mr. White could sit in a hotel to draw near to the Lord and spend time in the Word. Todd White has the same Holy Spirit as every believer. The key is relationship. You don't need some special anointing; you need a relationship with Jesus Christ. If you are filled with Holy Spirit, you are anointed. The Lord will draw near to you when you draw near to Him. Don't follow a man or a woman. Listen, yes. Learn, yes. But follow Jesus and always take the things you hear to our Father. We are to repent and be baptized in water and fire. Follow Jesus's lead, and you will find your path—the one He has laid out for you.

> **I baptize you with water for repentance. But after me comes one who is more powerful than I, whose sandals I am not worthy to carry. He will baptize you with the Holy Spirit and fire. (Matthew 3:11 NIV)**

It isn't about what God is doing through you but what He has done for you that is more important. I am not going to sit here and say that I have some super anointing or that I have some deep wisdom others do not. I won't say that I am so special and closer to God than others frankly because none of that is true. If you are a believer in Jesus Christ, what I will say is that this is far more than just saying some sinner's prayer that was created a few hundred years ago to get to heaven. We serve a living God who wants to draw near to us, but we have to make the decision to get our eyes off of this world—off of ourselves.

> **Move your heart closer and closer to God, and he will come even closer to you. But make sure you cleanse your life, you sinners, and keep your heart pure and stop doubting. Feel the pain of your sin, be sorrowful and weep! Let your joking around be turned into mourning and your joy into deep humiliation. Be willing to be made low before the Lord and he will exalt you! (James 4:8–10 TPT)**

He is telling us that coming to Him for just our wants is a selfish relationship. We have all had that one person who only reaches out when they want something. Imagine how our Father feels when we do the same to Him. Seek Him with a pure heart to know Him, and you will find Him there with open arms! However, I just encourage you to hold on tight because His plans for you are far greater than you can imagine! My prayer in sharing my testimony with you is that it encourages you to know, that you can know Him. You don't need someone to lay hands on you to draw near to Him. You don't need another sermon to draw near to Him. Don't get me wrong, there is a time we need prayer and hands laid on us. There are times we need deliverance and freedom, but I believe most of us just need self-discipline, not deliverance—replacing wrong thinking with right thinking by the renewal of our minds.

Do not conform to the pattern of this world, but be transformed by the renewing of your mind. Then you will be able to test and approve what God's will is—his good, pleasing and perfect will. (Romans 12:2 NIV)

Ask, and it will be given to you; seek, and you will find; knock, and it will be opened to you. For everyone who asks receives, and he who seeks finds, and to him who knocks it will be opened. (Matthew 7:7–8 NKJV)

Spring of 2019

The spring of 2019 was the absolute best semester we had at the house. There were ten of us and a one-year-old. We had so much fun with family game nights, gatherings that included sometimes, well, over eighty people. We had guest speakers come to the house and just miracles, signs, and wonders following us. There were many baptisms that followed after that first semester.

Most of us are still connected and pray for one another. I am so thankful for what the Lord did in this semester. During this semester, one of the girls told me I needed to watch the movie *The Heart of Man*. As I watched the movie, I was in tears. When it was over, I ran to my room and dropped to my knees.

I praised the Lord and thanked Him so much because it was during that beautiful documentary/movie that I realized God had delivered me from my sexual addiction. I hadn't thought about sex or masturbation in over a year and didn't even realize Jesus did that for me until that exact moment. It brought me to tears, and to this day, I am now over five years abstinent. That is something precious I'll save for my husband if God ever shows me that I'm to be married.

Dakota ended up having to get back to Indiana soon after he started school due to personal issues with his ex-girlfriend and daughter. Dorothy also returned to Indiana at the end of this semester as well. It was hard for Dorothy being away from home, and there were some challenges she and I had to allow the Lord to handle. Bree decided not to continue with school because she was offered a management position she didn't want to turn down. She remained active in our Bible studies and was always surrounded by students, friends, and many whom we consider family.

Fall of 2019

The fall of 2019 was one of the most challenging semesters. If you thought the first semester was stretching—nope, it was nothing compared to this semester of students at my house. The only thing I really want to share about this semester was the wonderful sisters in Christ who I gained. There was one young lady who stayed from the Spring of 2019 until I sold my house. I have so much love for her, and she is an amazing woman of God. I also met, who I consider one of my best friends, my dear sister from Switzerland. She came all the way to Texas seeking a better understanding of her identity, and she found it. She is and was and always will be so close to my heart. I truly did love everyone who came in and out of my home even if some of them didn't like me. I couldn't be more thankful for the process and the growth that helped me become the woman of God I am today. It was hard at times but so worth every step.

Spring of 2020

In the spring of 2020, well, pretty sure we all know what hit at this time. Before COVID shut down everything for a while, Bree and I were able to go on our very first ever vacation. We went on a cruise in February to the Bahamas. It was the *Impractical Joker* cruise, and it was a lot of fun. The girls who were renting rooms at the house had their challenges, kind of hard to be encouraged as an evangelist with all that was happening in the world. I don't want to get into the whole fear versus faith thing either. I honored what our government asked, and when the Lord said, "Go," or, "Pray," I obeyed Him and always will. All I will say is that a lot of the church was exposed and really spread a lot of hate more than the love of Jesus. However, God is faithful, and He loves His children! The semester had its challenges as well, but in April 2020, the Lord released me from Texas. In July 2020, I sold the house. Unexpectedly, He led me to a small town about fifteen minutes from where my daughter was born.

We tend to spend way too much time calling out the faults in others that we become blind and don't even recognize the judgment we are standing in.

> **Hypocrite! First get rid of the log in your own eye; then you will see well enough to deal with the speck in your friend's eye. (Matthew 7:5 NLT)**

I saw someone, who I consider a sister in Christ, post this on Facebook, and it is just the truth of what we see so much of today:

> *The Evangelist judging the Shepherd—He really needs to go out into the harvest and reach the lost. Why isn't he out there on the streets like me?*
>
> *The Shepherd judging the Evangelist—He is just leaving orphans out there on the streets. He needs to stay longer and disciple them like me.*
>
> *The Teacher judging the Prophet—He's all about spiritual things. We need sound doctrine. He needs to be studying the Word like me.*
>
> *The Prophet judging the Teacher—He needs to learn to hear God's voice not just read what God says. He really needs to stop being so religious and walk in the spirit like me.*
>
> *The Apostle judging them all—they really need to learn to be all things for all people like me.*
>
> *It's crazy how 5-fold was given for the equipping of the saints for the work of service and building up the body of Christ, yet members of the body wrongfully judge and criticize each other because they all are so different than each other, or they use this as titles to make themselves known instead of seeing the functions of the body to build the church. How twisted. We took that scripture about judging the body thinking it's righteous judgment to be critical of each other. Tearing each other down instead of truly judging righteously. Wake up church, you're beating up The Bride of Christ and I don't think you realize what you're doing! (Written by Tabitha Smith via Facebook)*

We need to remember what Paul wrote:

It's true that some are preaching out of jealousy and rivalry. But others preach about

Christ with pure motives. They preach because they love me, for they know I have been appointed to defend the Good news. Those others do not have pure motives as they preach about Christ. They preach with selfish ambition, not sincerely, intending to make my chains more painful to me. BUT THAT DOESN'T MATTER. WHETHER THEIR MOTIVES ARE FALSE OR GENUINE, THE MESSAGE ABOUT CHRIST IS BEING PREACHED EITHER WAY, SO I REJOICE. AND I WILL CONTINUE TO REJOICE. (Philippians 1:15–18 NLT)

Where am I now

I have lived in a little town in Ohio, right around the corner from the Indiana border for two years now. I have and do witness deliverances, healings, and freedom almost weekly. I have also had over forty baptisms in my bathtub here, all GLORY TO OUR KING. I have many people visiting, coming and going often. Some have lived with me; some I've just picked up off the street and brought home for a few days. God is still alive, He is still speaking, He is still loving, and He is still pursuing His children.

I share my testimony with almost everyone I meet. I share the Gospel of Jesus Christ with any ear that can hear. I have been blessed to travel to Switzerland and was invited to speak at a church there. I made my way to Ireland as well. I'm just open to all the Lord wants to do and will continue to follow Him all the days of my life. I haven't walked this out perfectly, and I probably never will. However, thank God it's not about perfection but about His grace. I know that I will never have to walk in any trial, good or bad, nor any path I take in this life will I be alone. I know whose I belong. I am a citizen of heaven.

My daughter, Bree, well, she met the man of her dreams. He's an amazing singer, songwriter, and musician. He was baptized, manifested, and delivered in July of 2022. He rose out of that water filled with Holy Spirit and received his prayer language. He is currently working on songs from his heart for the Lord. They were married about two weeks later. The wedding was incredible. On the previous Friday, I searched for a local photographer to capture the wedding for us. When I found one, the woman agreed to come to the house on the wedding day, which was that Sunday. Once she arrived, I walked her around and introduced her to everyone, all while sharing the Gospel and some of my testimony. The photographer stated she had been seeking the Lord and really wanted to be baptized. I expressed that I had a baptism tank and that if she really wanted to give her life to Christ, I would be privileged and blessed to walk her through that. She then expressed she would not want to take away from the kids on their wedding day, I simply grinned and said, 'Come, let's talk to them.' My daughter and son-in-law were so excited and shared that it would be the perfect wedding gift. So, after the ceremony, still in the wedding dress and tuxedo, we gathered as a family and baptized our photographer. Soon after, the best man decided he too, wanted to give his life to Christ. It was the most amazing wedding day I have ever been a part of. Dakota, well, he's still my butthead little brother, but I love him dearly. He is no longer dependent on insulin and is working a really good job he enjoys. He was also baptized by his niece, my daughter, in April of 2022. My brother, son-in-law, and beautiful daughter all live right next door to me, which I simply love.

As for my mom, I struggled with trying to be in a relationship with her for years. In December of 2021, she was telling people that I was diagnosed as bipolar and schizophrenic, but I was in a car accident and forgot. I honestly have no idea where she came up with that. She also tells people that I prey on elders in churches, and that I force people off the streets and "make them" get baptized. When I called to confront her about the things she was saying, she just yelled at me. I ended up telling her that it wasn't healthy for me to continue in a relationship with her, but I love her and have a heart that someday the Lord will restore us. I pray for her often and haven't spoken to her since. I am still blocked on her social media, along with my daughter and my little brother now.

And last, but certainly not least, my beautiful sister Dorothy. When I moved here, we were finally close enough again and able to spend our holidays together. Dorothy came to the house often, and I to hers. In November of 2021, Dorothy was diagnosed with a rare form of thyroid cancer that had spread all over her body. I was blessed with the privilege and honor to be her caregiver for the last months of her life. She shined the most beautiful light and touched so many people in her lifetime. It was encouraging and heartbreaking all at the same time to see a woman live the true definition of the scripture:

For to me, to live is Christ and to die is gain. (Philippians 1:21 NIV)

Even with her last breath, Dorothy was praising the Lord. She went home to be with Father on December 28, 2021, at 9:11 a.m. She will never be forgotten and is missed every single day.

He who dwells in the secret place of the Most High Shall abide under the shadow of the Almighty. (Psalm 91:1 NKJV)

Let the inner movement of your heart always be to love one another, and never play the role of an actor wearing a mask. Despise evil and embrace everything that is good and virtuous. Be devoted to tenderly loving your fellow believers as members of one family. Try to outdo yourselves in respect and honor of one another. (Romans 12:9–10 TPT)

One thing Dorothy kept repeating to me in her last weeks was, "Zara, don't forget to just enjoy being His." That has echoed in my spirit since. We spend far too much time allowing our differences to divide us, rather than grow us. It amazes me how if you don't come into agreement with someone, they will just cut you off.

As if love doesn't look like being honest! As if love means we cater to one another's emotions.

So, what if someone does not agree with me, doesn't mean you can't love me! So, what if I do not agree with you, doesn't mean I can't love you! Seriously, we need to stop living so selfishly and acting like love means we are always in agreement. Too much time is wasted on hate and division because we put our opinions above others. It is honestly heartbreaking.

If we spent half the time, we did on seeking the wrong in someone, we would find there's a person Jesus paid the ultimate price for! Oh, how I want to love the way Father does…love holds no account of wrongs. That doesn't mean love is always in agreement with decisions or actions. It means love, loves enough to say something, with love, and still be able to love. It's not a mushy feeling and butterflies. As I've said before, that's worldly and like butterflies, soon flies away!!!

God created all of us differently. There's always room to humble ourselves and grow through our differences. Not pointing fingers, cutting people off, running away, picking up offense because someone doesn't agree with us, but to truly pray for one another, love without contingency, and still stand in what we believe without it dividing us! Jesus ate with the sinners, broken, lost, not because He was in agreement with them, but because He loved them. He loves us and is our example. Perhaps, today is the day to make the decision to follow Him, to follow His lead, to follow His example! The choice is and always will be yours.

I pray that my testimony encourages you to get alone and draw near to the LIVING GOD, who absolutely adores and loves you. Jesus Christ knows you and wants you to come with a pure heart. That doesn't mean you clean yourself up! It means even with your junk, you seek Him for real with all your heart, mind, and soul. You seek Him and don't ever stop. He will draw near as you draw near to HIM. I pray God's divine favor overwhelms you, and you see yourself the way that OUR FATHER SEES YOU!

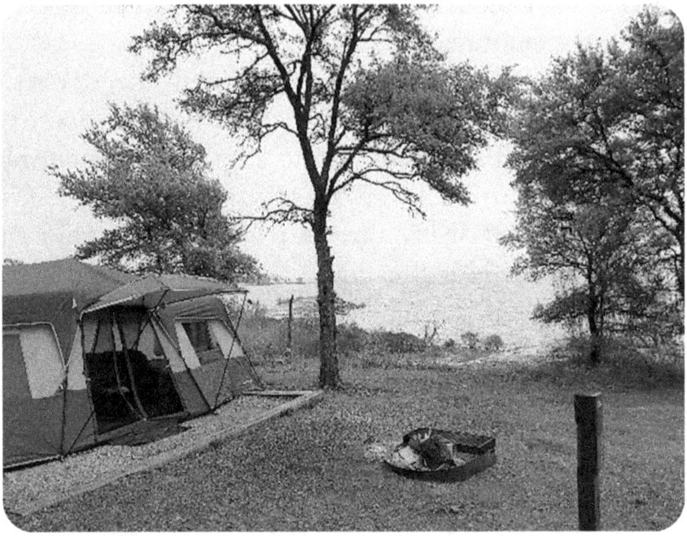

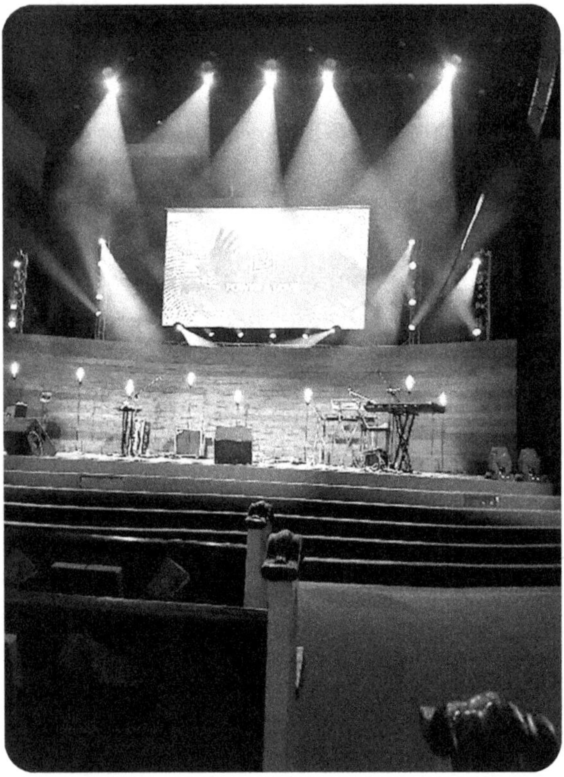

Danny Herman
WE PAY FOR
EXPERIENCE
NOW HIRING
Isaiah 40:31
TRUST
17326

TOBY MAC
ARENA

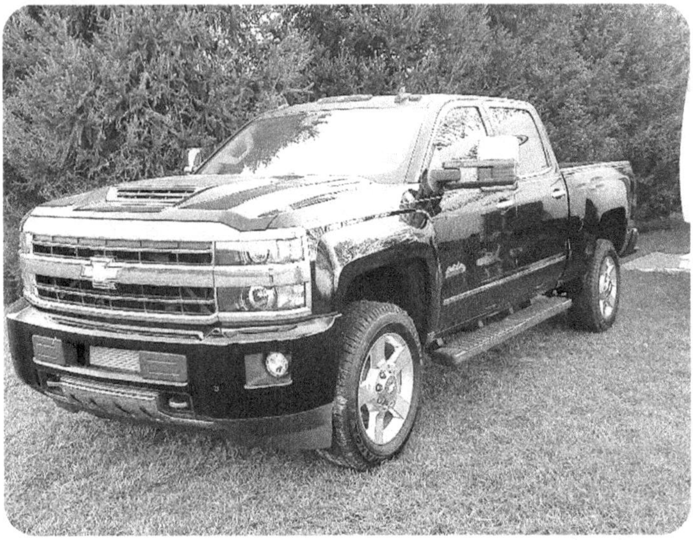

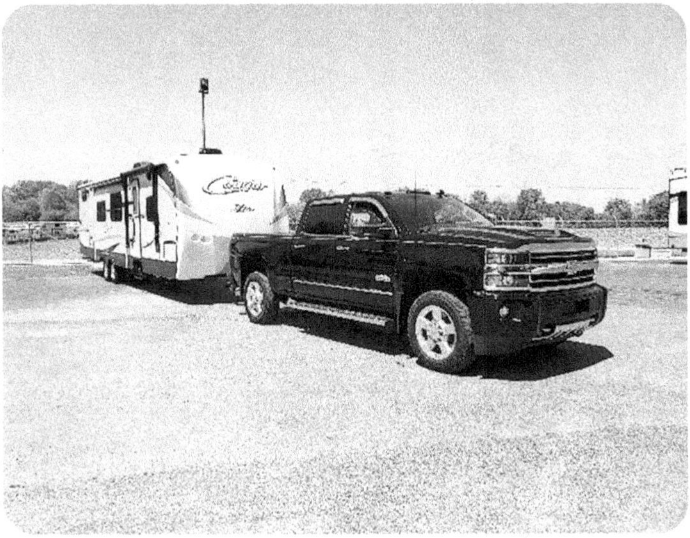
Cougar

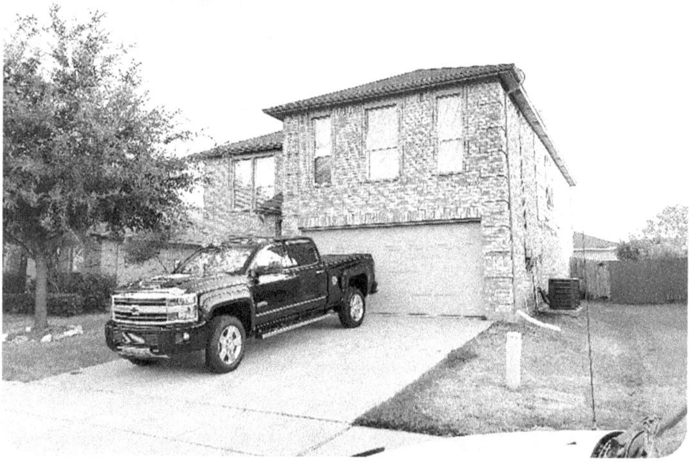

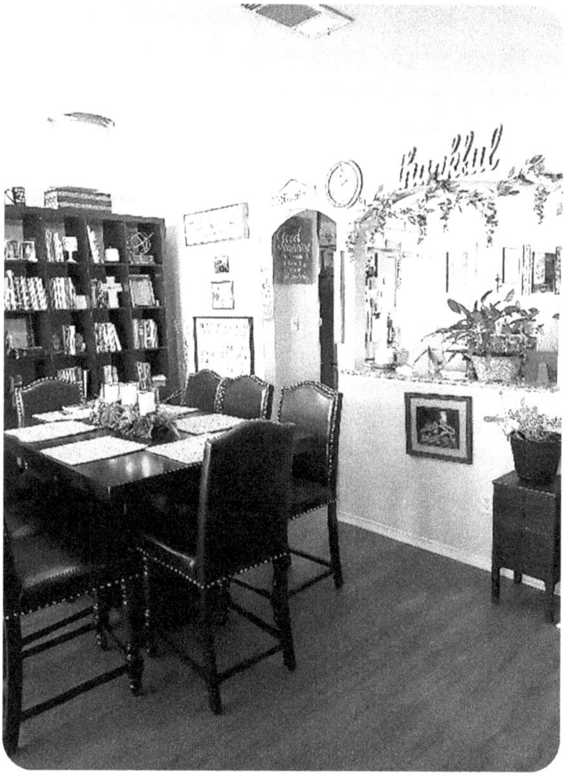

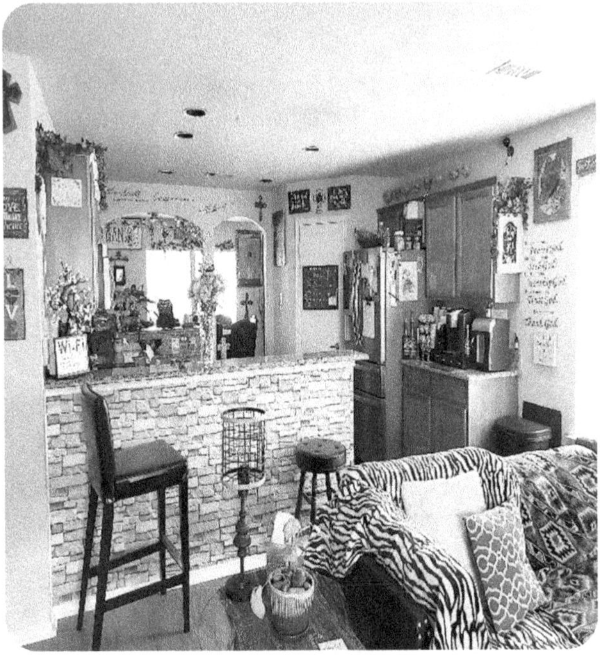

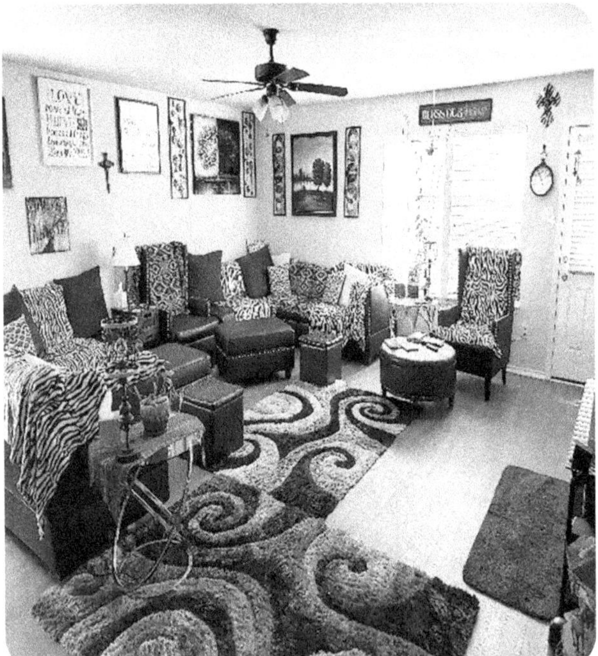

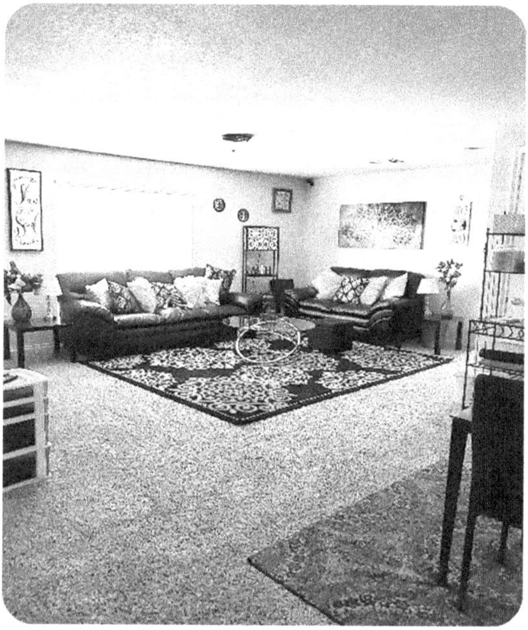

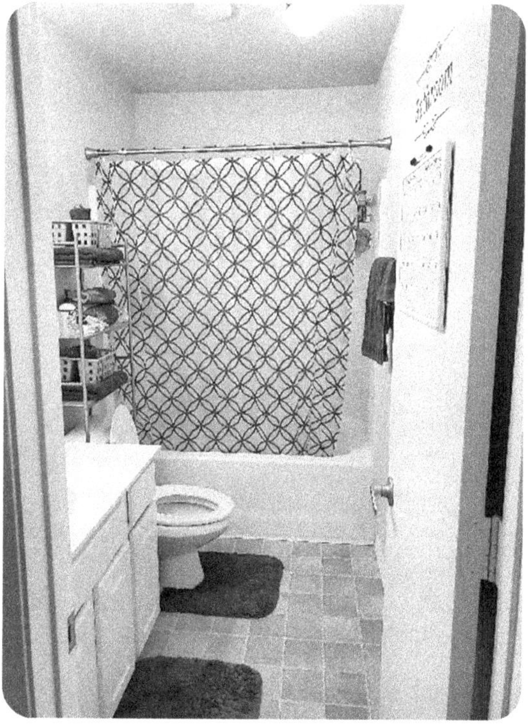

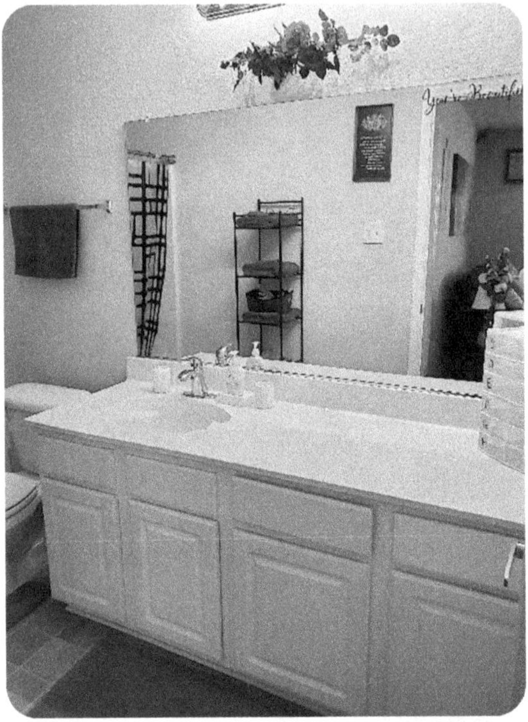

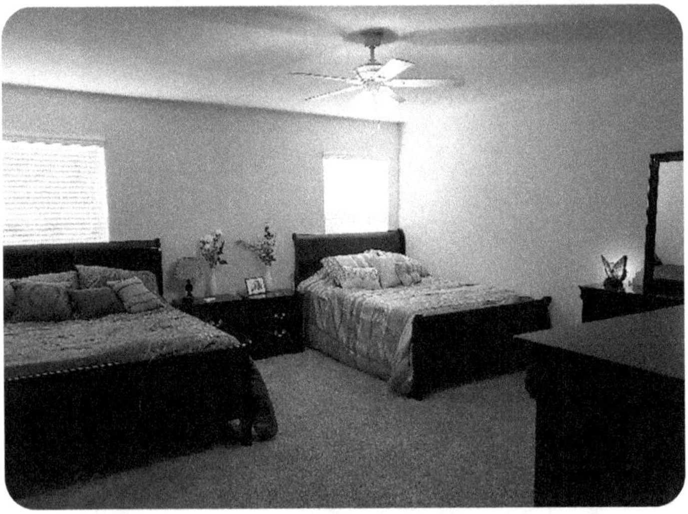

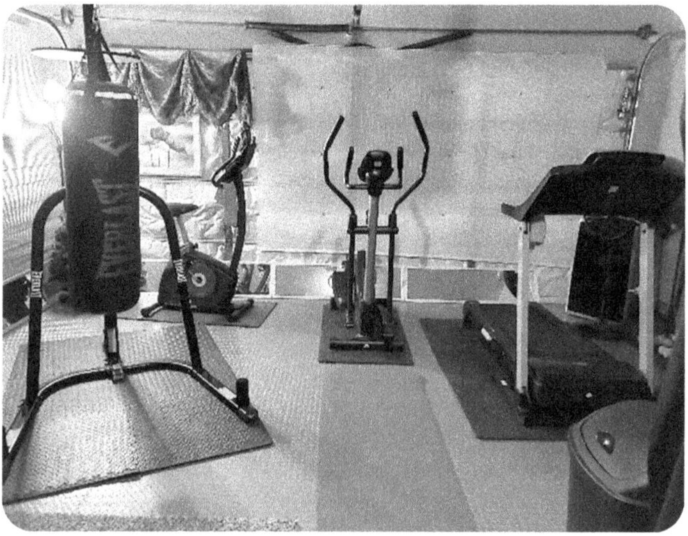

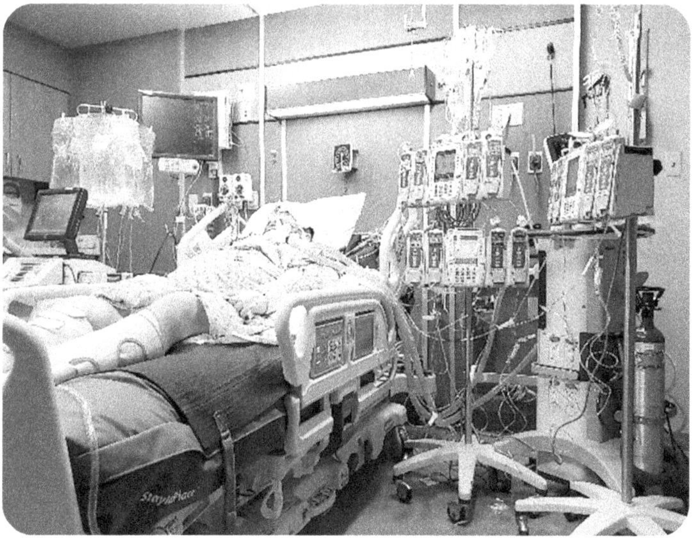

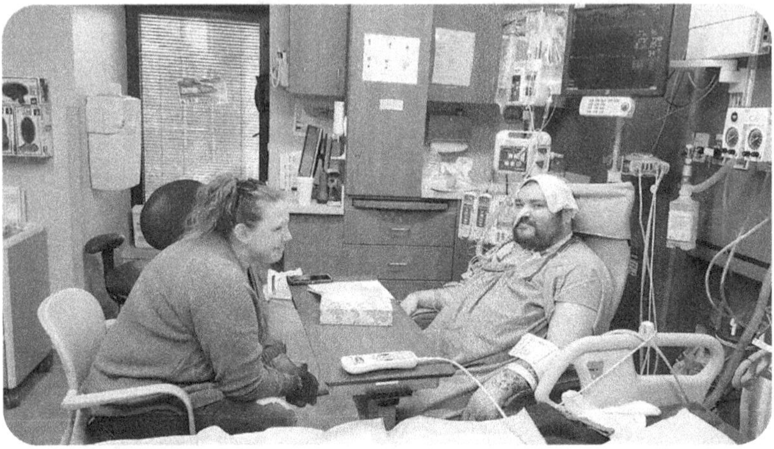

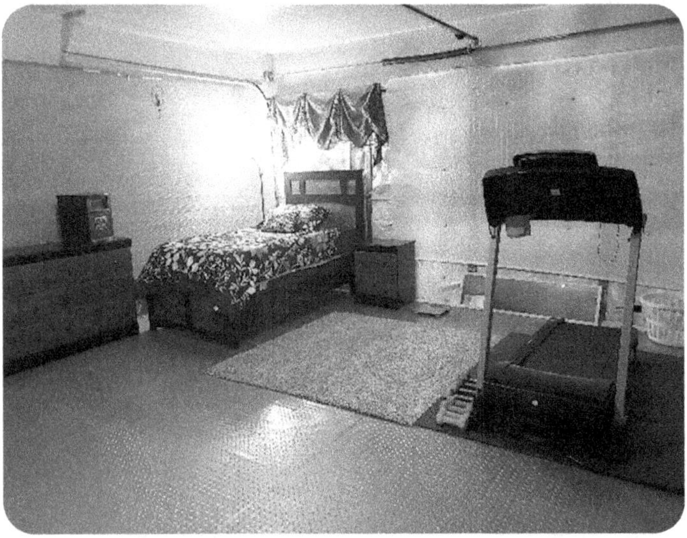

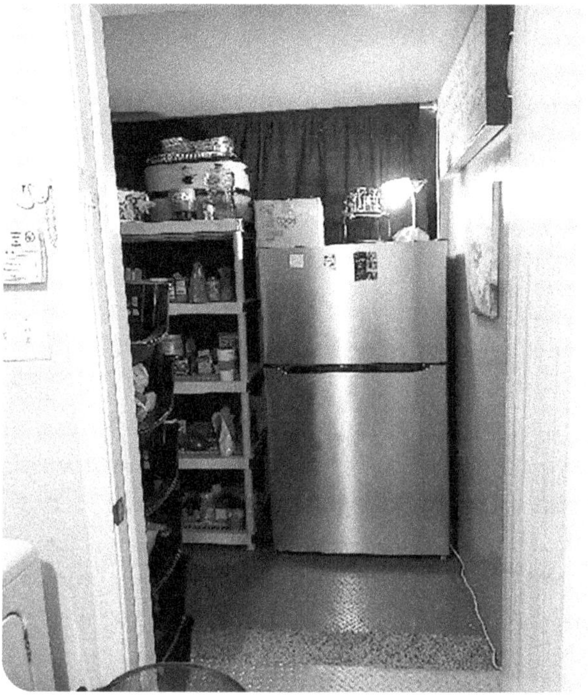

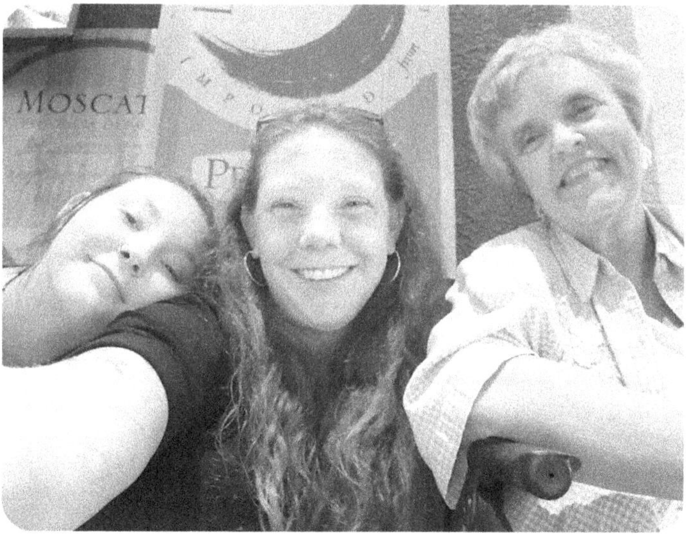
MOSCAT

ABOUT THE AUTHOR

Born in Michigan, Kyna Bryn is a mother, author, ordained minister, speaker, and follower of Jesus Christ. Ms. Bryn is a confident encourager who continues to remain rooted in the Word of God. She is a very direct woman who lovingly cares for and about others. Ms. Bryn now advocates for the broken, lost, and abandoned. It is her heart to share with others the message of not having to be a victim and that we can rise up from the ashes, completely victorious. Now residing in Ohio, Ms. Bryn continues to share the Gospel and good news of Jesus Christ with those who have ears to hear (kynabryn.com).